COLLINS POCKET REFERENCE

WHISKY

Carol P. Shaw

HarperCollins*Publishers*

HarperCollins Publishers
PO Box, Glasgow G4 0NB

First published 1996

Reprint 10 9 8 7 6 5 4 3 2 1 0

© HarperCollins Publishers, 1996

ISBN 0 00 472018 0

A catalogue record for this book is available from the British Library

Printed and bound in Italy by Rotolito Lombarda S.p.A., Pioltello.

Contents

The History of Scotch Whisky-making

*I*t is widely accepted that whisky has been distilled in Scotland for hundreds of years, and different hypotheses as to its origins have been suggested. Some state that it was brought into the country by missionary monks from Ireland; others point out that, as the Arabs were among the first to learn distillation techniques, knights and men returning from the Crusades could have brought the knowledge back with them. It may well be, however, that it evolved simply as a means of using up barley which would otherwise have been ruined after a wet harvest.

The name itself is derived from the Gaelic, *uisge beatha*, meaning 'water of life'. The Latin equivalent, *aqua vitae*, was a term which was commonly used throughout Europe to describe the local spirit. *Aqua vitae* made its first appearance in official Scottish records in 1494, with the record of malt being sold to one Friar

John Cor with which to make the spirit, but *uisge* seems to have first been mentioned in the account of the funeral and wake of a Highland chieftain around 1618. The amount of whisky making throughout Scotland increased greatly during the seventeenth century, and nowhere more so than in the Highlands. In fact, so enthusiastic was the growth in distillation that before the end of the sixteenth century there had already been complaints in Parliament that so much barley was being used in whisky production that it was in short supply as a foodstuff! These distillers' method was basic and simple: a sack of barley might be soaked in water – for example, in a burn – for a day or two, then the barley would be spread

out in a dry place, allowing it to sprout, for around 10 days. The sprouting would be halted by drying the barley over a peat fire (peat being used as the main source of fuel in the Highlands). It was then put in a container with boiling water and yeast, to ferment. This mix would be passed twice through a pot still, emerging as whisky at the other end. These distillers had to be fairly skilled at their job, to possess the judgement to know when to take off the middle cut of the spirit (the drinkable part), avoiding the poisonous foreshots, at the start of the distillation, and the lower-quality feints, or aftershots, at the end. Although they had no instruments, methods did evolve of testing the whisky's strength, including setting fire to the spirit to measure the amount of liquid left behind, and mixing it with gunpowder to see how it reacted when ignited – if the gunpowder-and-whisky cocktail exploded, it was known that the whisky was too strong!

It was during the seventeenth century, too, that the first tax on whisky was introduced by Parliament, because of the pressing need to raise revenue to finance the army fighting in the English Civil War in 1644. Although it was reduced under the Commonwealth, this episode effectively marked the beginning of the principle of the taxation of whisky.

The union of Scotland and England in 1707, however, heralded some changes for the whisky industry, and few of them were constructive. A malt tax was introduced in 1725 which adversely affected the quality of beer – until then the most popular drink – and of whiskies produced by the professional commercial distillers in the more populous Lowlands, who were obliged to produce whiskies of poorer quality, with less malted barley content. These taxes also applied to Highland malt whisky, but in that still-inaccessible region it was much easier to ignore, and illicit distillation continued to flourish. This attempt at revenue raising, affecting the Lowland distillers but ignored in the Highlands, set a pattern for the rest of the century.

Sir Edward Landseer's somewhat romanticised view of an illicit still in the Highlands (United Distillers)

The large distillers in the Lowlands continued successfully to produce rough grain whisky whose quantity was more important than its quality, for consumption locally and in England, where it was often used as a basis for cheap gin. However, pressure from the English distillers, who were being undercut by Scottish imports flooding the market, encouraged Parliament to introduce a series of increasingly draconian taxes against the Scots whisky. The small distillers in the Highlands – most of whom were probably farmers and crofters, pursuing a lucrative sideline – continued to make superior quality whisky without paying tax. Much of this whisky was brought to the Lowlands for sale, where it was more popular with those who could afford it than the rougher spirit produced by the Lowland distillers. The government in London had no answer to the problems they had helped create in the whisky industry, other than to raise taxes still further, making the law seem more and more ineffectual.

Finally, however, pressure on the government brought an abandonment of its futile attempts at taxation and regulation. A Royal Commission was set up to investigate the industry, the Excise service in the Highlands was strengthened, and in 1822 an act was passed which brought harsher penalties for those found to be operating unlicensed stills. The following year the Excise Act made an attempt to encourage licensed distilling, cutting both duty and restrictions on exports to England. Now, an annual licence of £10 was introduced on stills over forty gallons (smaller stills were not allowed), and a more modest duty of 2/3d per gallon of whisky brought in. The Duke of Gordon, whose estates included the Glenlivet area, was a prime mover in the reforms, and he encouraged his tenants, including George Smith, producer of the whisky which came to be known as The Glenlivet, to take out licences. The new act was effective and successful, and the amount of legally distilled whisky consumed had risen threefold by 1827.

Freed from its legislative shackles, the whisky industry was able to concentrate on the development of its product and markets. The product itself was given an impetus by the invention by Aeneas Coffey, an Irish former exciseman, of a new still which he patented in 1832; this allowed the distillation of grain whisky to take place in a continuous process in one still. The new process cut back on costs, allowing the Lowland grain distillers to use even less malted barley than before, and to produce on an even bigger scale. Ironically, however, the success of the Excise Act and the new patent still brought trouble for the industry during the mid nineteenth century, because of overproduction and despite the exploiting of new export markets in the Empire and overseas. This development saw the foreshadowing of the emergence of the Distillers Company, with the combining in a price-fixing cartel of the six biggest Lowland grain whisky producers; they were not to join together officially, however, until 1877, by which time the face of the industry had changed dramatically.

This change was brought about by the development of techniques of blending malt and grain whiskies to produce a lighter spirit than the traditional single malt, and a more flavoursome one than grain whisky. In the 1850s Andrew Usher, the Edinburgh whisky merchant who was agent for the

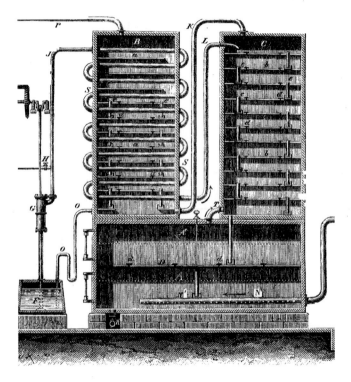

A detail from an 1870 illustration showing the internal workings of the Coffey Still

Glenlivet whiskies, had vatted together several casks of Glenlivet from his stocks, producing in the process a more consistent product. The practice was soon extended to the blending of malt and grain. This was held to produce a lighter spirit which English drinkers, unused to the much stronger malt product of the pot still, found much more palatable. It also introduced an element of

Andrew Usher, first chairman of the North British Distillery Co. and a pioneer of blending

consistency to the product. Coincidentally, this development came when reserves of brandy, the first-choice spirit in England, were threatened as a result of the Phylloxera blight in the French vineyards in the 1860s. Timely exploitation of the market in England by the grain producers and blenders meant that, as stocks of brandy declined in the 1870s and '80s, the new blended whiskies came to take their place as the quality spirit, and the 1890s was a period of unprecedented growth for the Scottish whisky industry. New malt distilleries were opened and groups like Distillers and the North British Distillery Company, serving the interests of the grain distillers and the blenders respectively, became phenomenally successful. The whisky industry was developing to become recognizable as the industry it is today.

The boom period was followed, typically, by a slump, and difficult times for the industry at the beginning of this century were compounded by the First World War and the introduction of Prohibition in the USA in 1920. The years from then to the Second World War saw a drop in output of almost 50%, and an almost complete halt being brought to the production of malt whisky. This situation continued after the war when, naturally, what grain was available had to be diverted to feed the people rather than make whisky. As prosperity returned in the 1950s, whisky output increased and exports rose. New distilleries were built in the 1960s, old ones reopened, and the production of malt whisky quadrupled in a decade. Take-over and consolidation were the keynotes of the industry in the 1970s, with English brewers moving into the whisky market on a large scale. This trend culminated in the messy take-over of the Distillers Company (now United Distillers) by Guinness, a transaction which resulted in the chairman of the brewing giant and several of his advisers ending up in court. Ironically, however, the adage of there being no bad publicity seems to be borne out by the Distillers take-over: an episode which apparently brought the industry into disrepute, came at a time when the market was picking up again after the slump lasting from the mid '70s to the mid '80s, and served to give whisky a timely publicity boost.

This upturn in the drink's fortunes continued into the 1990s, with the emphasis in marketing being placed on quality rather than quantity: cheaper blends have tended to

Lochranza Distillery on the Isle of Arran. Opened in 1995, it is Scotland's newest distillery (Isle of Arran Distiller Ltd)

disappear, single malts are taking an increasing share of the market, and price rises are being met by consumers, who seem to prefer the new expensive-and-exclusive image of the drink. Increasing importance was placed on packaging and advertising, and with the marketing of new visitor centres in the distilleries themselves as tourist attractions in their own right. By 1995, however, growth in the Scotch market as a whole had slowed once again and the industry was having to work hard to maintain its position. The premium end of the industry continued to be healthy (helped no doubt by the first reduction in excise duty for a hundred years) although the mass-market sector faced increasing competition, particularly from vodka producers. It responded by the creation of whisky-based drinks designed to appeal to a younger, less traditional customer base – whiskies spiked with red chilli peppers, for example – but the long-term success of these remains to be seen. Perhaps the biggest challenge facing the drinks industry as it moves towards the new millennium is the abandonment of duty-free facilities within the European Union in 1999; this will be a particularly harsh blow to the Scotch producers to whom the duty-free market is worth some £80 million. The industry has faced other crises before and it will undoubtedly survive this one and flourish once more – something which can only be good for all those who appreciate and love good whisky.

How Scotch Whisky is Made

*T*wo different processes are used for the distillation of Scotch malt and grain whiskies.

Malt whisky

In malt whisky distillation, there are several basic steps to the process: malting, mashing, fermentation, distillation and maturation, although the minor elements may vary from one distillery to another. Barley may be bought in pre-malted, but if it is not, it is first filtered to remove any foreign matter.

(1) **Malting**. The process begins when the barley is transferred to soak in tanks of water which go by the self-explanatory name of barley steeps; this process takes two to four days. In the traditional process, the barley is then spread on a malting floor, to be turned by hand daily for the next twelve days or so, allowing it to sprout; now, however, most distilleries use mechanical devices for turning the sprouting barley. As the seeds germinate, the starch in the barley releases some of its sugars. At the appropriate moment, germination is stopped by drying the cereal in a malt kiln over a peat furnace or fire. The peat smoke which flavours the drying barley at this stage can, depending on its intensity, be tasted in the final whisky itself. The malt kilns traditionally had the pagoda-style roofs which were such an instantly recognizable characteristic of the malt distilleries; these can still be seen on older distilleries.

(2) **Mashing**. The next stage for the malted barley is passage

Turning the barley by hand on a traditional malting floor (Scotch Whisky Association)

through a mill, from which it emerges roughly ground as grist. From here it is moved to a mash tun, a large vat where it is mixed with hot water and agitated, so that its sugars dissolve to produce wort, a sweet, non-alcoholic liquid. This process is repeated to ensure that all the sugars have been collected. The solid remains of the barley are removed at this point for conversion to cattle food.

(3) **Fermentation**. The wort is cooled and transferred to washbacks, large vats where yeast is added and the process of fermentation begins. The chemical reaction which takes place with the addition of the yeast converts the sugars in the wort to alcohol, a process which takes around two days and results in a low-strength alcoholic liquid now called wash.

A traditional pagoda-topped malting kiln (Scotch Whisky Association)

Washbacks where the wort is fermented to produce the wash (Scotch Whisky Association)

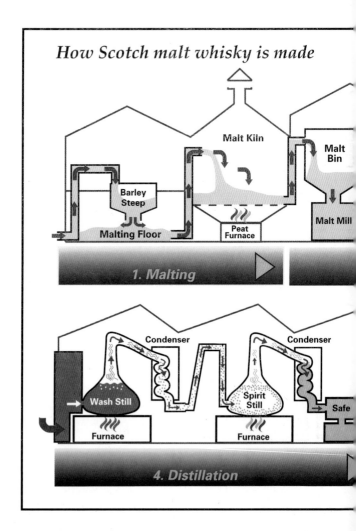

How Scotch malt whisky is made

Malt Kiln

Malt Bin

Barley Steep

Malting Floor

Peat Furnace

Malt Mill

1. Malting

Condenser

Condenser

Wash Still

Spirit Still

Safe

Furnace

Furnace

4. Distillation

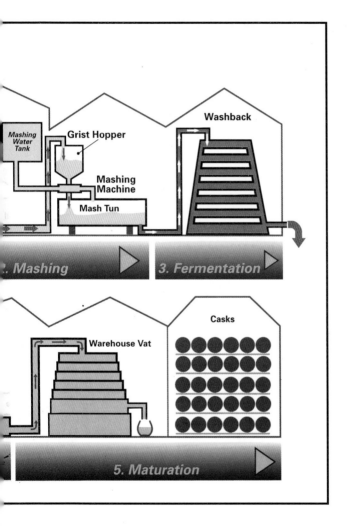

(4) **Distillation.** The wash is then ready for the stills. The shape of the still is one of the most important factors in the whisky-making process, as it can have a decisive influence on the final character of the malt whisky: for instance, a still with a short neck will produce a whisky with heavier oils and a more intense flavour, whereas lighter-flavoured whiskies with less heavy oils will emerge from a still with a long or high neck. The first still which the wash passes through is known, appropriately, as the wash still, and here it is heated.

As the alcohol has a lower boiling point than water, the alcoholic steam rises up the still through its long spout to the worm, a condensing coil. The distillate, now called low wines, is passed into the second still, the spirit still, where the process is repeated, with the liquid running off into the glass-fronted spirit safe.

It is at this point that the skill of the distiller is crucial: unable to smell or taste the liquid to judge it, he must know when to separate the middle cut, or main run

Copper wash stills (Scotch Whisky Association)

Drawing a sample of new whisky from the spirit sample safe (Glenturret Distillery Ltd)

of the spirit, which contains the best-quality alcohol needed for malt whisky, from the foreshots (the raw, poisonous first distillate) and the feints, or aftershots, which contain a lower grade of alcohol. Once separated, foreshots and feints are fed back into the wash for redistillation.

(5) **Maturation**. The main run of the alcohol is now transferred for storage to a vat and is mixed with water to bring it down in strength. It is then transferred into casks for maturing. The whole process of distillation can theoretically be completed inside a week, but the whisky must now mature for at least three years before it can be sold; during this time, a small percentage of the whisky, known as the 'angels' share', will evaporate. In practice, malt whiskies are left to mature for an average of eight to fifteen years.

Maturing casks (Glenturret Distillery Ltd)

Grain whisky

With the exception of the Invergordon Distillery, all grain distilleries are located in the Lowlands. Grain distilleries use patent (or Coffey) stills, which can operate continuously. The basic process used is similar to that for malt, up to the point of distillation, although everything takes place on a much larger scale, and with much less malted barley: maize, unmalted barley or other cereals are generally used.

Distillation is carried out in two large cylindrical columns which are linked by pipes. The wash passes into the first column, the rectifier, in a coiled pipe running through its length. Jets of steam are forced up into the column, through a series of perforated plates between which the coiled pipe passes, heating the wash inside before it passes out and into the analyser. In the analyser the wash is no longer in the coiled pipe, and it is now met by another jet of steam passing through more perforated plates. The steam and evaporated alcohol rise and are passed back into the rectifier, with the alcohol cooling as it moves up, encountering fresh, cold wash in the coiled pipe on its way down, until it reaches a cold water coil where it condenses before passing out of the still. The impure alcohols in the first and last part of the distillate can be redistilled, while the alcohol which reaches the spirit safe and receiver is very pure. The whisky will mature faster than malt, and is less subject to variable factors. The vast majority of the produce will go for blending not long after its three-year maturation period has passed.

Blending

*B*lending is a slightly separate part of the whisky-making process, with a third product being made from malt and grain whiskies. It both guarantees consistency of the brand and aims to create a new whisky of character in its own right. It is a process which absorbs the greater part of the distilleries' production, and is the mainstay of the industry.

The process was developed on a commercial footing in the second half of the nineteenth century. Although it may initially have been used as a way of stretching further supplies of the more expensive malt whisky, it was the means by which whisky was popularized first in the English market, then overseas.

The blender at work (Scotch Whisky Association and overleaf)

Blending is an olfactory craft, with blenders nosing rather than tasting whiskies. It is a highly skilled profession, with anything from 20 to 50 different whiskies being mixed in any one brand, including varieties of type, region, distillery and age. The new whisky's character is dependent on how well these different component whiskies complement and contrast with one another to bring out their various flavours. The high number of component whiskies is the blender's guarantee of consistency: if one contributing distillery goes out of production, the consistency of the blend can be maintained more easily than if there were a lesser number of whiskies, each with a stronger presence, as ingredients.

The ingredients and their proportions are closely guarded secrets, although it is generally assumed that where a blender owns a distillery, the distillery's produce will be represented to some degree in the blend: so, for example, the produce of Laphroaig Distillery, which is owned by Allied Distillers, is present in their Long John, Ballantine's and Teacher's blends. The produce of some distilleries is never bottled as a single malt, and goes entirely for blending.

After the whiskies are matured, they are mixed together in their correct proportions in a vat, then 'married' in oak casks for at least a year to allow intermingling and further maturation to take place. As with most malts, the blend is reduced to the correct strength by the addition of water. Burnt-sugar caramel may be added to bring a blend up to its desired colour before the whisky is filtered, bottled and labelled.

Different Types of Scotch Whisky

*T*here are particular legal constraints on what can be termed Scotch whisky, the most basic of which dictate the components of the whisky (cereals, malt and yeast), the maximum alcoholic strength at distillation (94.8% alcohol by volume), and the minimum length of maturation (at least three years). Finally, the whisky itself must have been distilled and matured in Scotland.

Scotland produces two main types of whisky, and all the available varieties of the spirit are variations on these themes. The first is malt whisky, made from malted barley, using a pot still; and the second is grain whisky, made from other cereals – maize or unmalted barley, together with a little malted barley – in a patent still. The two types' distillation processes are explained on pp. 19–27; what follows here is an explanation of the varieties in which they are available.

Single malt is the product of one distillery. Legally, it can be sold after only three years' maturation, but in practice it is generally left to mature from between eight to fifteen years, by which time its character and flavour has become more pronounced and rounded. Generally, whiskies of varying proof strengths and ages from different casks are mixed together, ensuring a consistent distillery product (as the product of any one distillation will inevitably not be identical to any other), although the age which appears on the label is always the age of the youngest distillation in the bottle. Malts are diluted from their cask strength (up to mid 60s percentage alcohol by volume) to 40% or 43% for commercial marketing. Single malts comprise a relatively small, although increasing, proportion of the total whisky market.

A sub-group of single malt whisky is the **single-cask malt**. Generally available commercially only through specialist shops and independent merchants (see pp. 49–51), these are whiskies which, as the name suggests, are the produce of one distillation, bottled straight from the cask and not vatted with any other produce from the distillery. This process, together with the absence of chill filtration before the whiskies are bottled, ensures that the particular character of a distillery's whisky – and, indeed, of a specific distillation – is unmasked, and greatly emphasized. Supplies of a particular variety or distillation are, by nature, finite. This is the most expensive type of whisky, often costing at least double the price of a normal, distillery-bottled single malt, but felt by many whisky drinkers to be well worth the expense.

A **vatted malt** is the final of the malt whisky sub-groups. This type of whisky has a long pedigree, having formed the basis of the first blended whisky in the mid nineteenth century. Vatted malts are normally produced by blenders and big companies who have a variety of malt distilleries from which to take their product. It could be regarded as a half-way house between a blend and a single malt, although the flavours in some vatted malts can be just as well developed as those in a single. Single malts of different distilleries and different ages are mixed together, the age (if any) on the label being that of the youngest whisky in the mixture. The words 'vatted malt' normally do not appear on a label; instead, the absence of the word 'single' before 'malt', together with an absence of a distillery name, is generally an indicator of a vatted malt.

Grain whisky has been mentioned briefly above, and in proportion to the quantities in which it is produced, very little of it is bottled in its own right. Instead, its main function is as a component part of a blend. **Blended whiskies** are a mixture of malt and grain, not necessarily in any fixed proportions but rather in a recipe which will achieve the blender's desired balance in terms of character, cost and quality. Blends were the means in the nineteenth century by which hitherto too-strongly flavoured malt whiskies were mellowed for the palate in markets outside Scotland – firstly for England, then for export markets. The desired aim of a blender is not to dilute or diminish the flavours of the various component whiskies, but rather to choose ones which are both compatible and complementary, resulting in the creation of a new whisky of distinctive character. In this way, consistency of the product can also be assured. Blended whiskies, of which there are over a thousand, comprise the greater part of the whisky market. The major blenders generally own both malt and grain distilleries, so it is safe to assume that the product of a particular malt distillery will be represented to some degree in its owner's blends.

A **de luxe whisky** is a particular type of blend, recognized to be of superior quality to a standard blend. De luxe whiskies generally contain a higher proportion of malt which is older, more mature and consequently more expensive. Some de luxes carry an age statement on their label; as with other whiskies, this is the age of the youngest component in the bottle.

Blends, but of a quite different type, is a name which can be given to the growing market for whisky **liqueurs**. Some of these contain whisky flavoured with honey, fruits, herbs and spices, while the cream liqueurs also contain whisky, but are more inclined towards cream, coffee and chocolate in their flavours.

Regional Characteristics
of Scotch Malt Whisky

*T*he qualities and characteristics associated with particular producing regions are not a result of current tastes and fashions, but rather a legacy of the past. In times when roads were often poor or, at some times of the year, non-existent, when communications were often difficult, sometimes dangerous and always time-consuming, and trade between different parts of the country was expensive, it was obvious that a distillery would use the raw materials and ingredients which were to hand in a particular locality rather than go to the trouble of importing produce from other areas. These factors, combined with local climate and geology, helped produce whiskies which varied in character from one part of the country to another.

The current chief distinction, between Highland and Lowland whiskies, is also a legacy of a past legal and fiscal policy. As a means of controlling the trade and movement of whisky from the Highlands to the Lowlands (whose cheaper, coarser grain spirit was then successfully being exported into England), the Highland dividing line was established, following roughly the Highland Boundary Fault Line, which runs from the Firth of Clyde to the Firth of Tay. The distinction remained, even with the equalizing of quality between malts from north and south of the line, and is still recognized today. The maps on pp. 38–39 and 42–43 show all existing distilleries within the broad categorizations that follow.

Lowland malts are defined as those coming from the southern half of Scotland – that is, from south of the Highland line. In terms of their taste, the Lowland malts are perhaps a good first stepping stone into the wider world of malt whiskies for the drinker who wants to graduate from blends: relatively unassertive in character, they are generally soft and light, with a gentle sweetness which ensures them many fans among more experienced palates. Much of the produce of the Lowland malt distilleries is used in blends.

As a once-popular music-hall ditty more colourfully suggested, **Campbeltown** was a major centre of whisky production. Over twenty distilleries operated there in the later nineteenth century, encouraged by the abundance of local supplies of peat, barley from the Mull of Kintyre, and a nearby source of cheap coal. However, over-production, too-wide variations in quality and the exhaustion of the local coal seam contributed to the decline of the local industry, to the point where only two distilleries now remain. With the shift in emphasis from sea-borne to road traffic, it is unlikely that the town will ever again regain its former eminence. Nevertheless, it still retains its regional classification. Campbeltown whiskies are generally accepted to be quite distinctive, with a character which is mellower than that of the Islay malts, with a smoothness and a variable peatiness in the flavour.

Islay malts must be, for everyone from the beginner to the connoisseur, the most distinctive of all single malt whiskies – certainly, their flavour is among the strongest of all the regions. Peat is the key, both in terms of its influence on the ingredients used for distillation and of its presence in the final

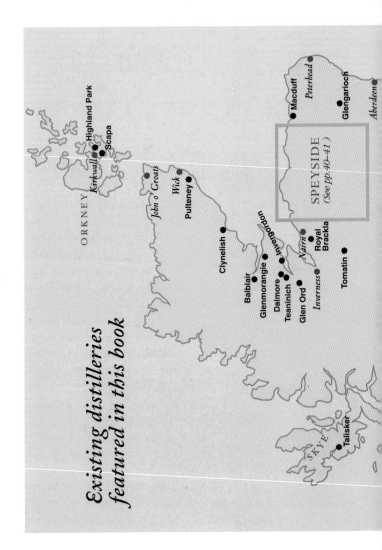

Existing distilleries featured in this book

taste. The island has extensive beds of peat, over which the water used in the distillation process flows, arriving at its destination already flavoured. Varying amounts of peat are also used to dry the barley. In the past this latter ingredient, too, was produced locally, although now it may be brought in. Peat is noticeable in the flavours of all the Islay malts, from the mildest to the most intensely flavoured, imparting a dryness which is sometimes balanced by sweetness, sometimes emphasized by smokiness. For beginners to single malts, the Islay whiskies seem like an acquired taste, but they are an essential ingredient in the whisky-blending process, and the chances are that what you may think of as the distinctively Scottish flavour in your whisky is imparted by their presence in a blend.

Finally, the largest region, with more distilleries than the rest of the country combined, is **Highland,** probably the quintessential Scottish whisky production area. This is the land which lies to the north of the Highland line and includes distilleries as far apart as Inchmurrin in Dunbartonshire, Oban in Argyll, Pulteney in Wick and Highland Park in Orkney. As might be expected across such a wide area, generalizations become less valid and sub-division becomes more necessary. Geographical divisions of north, south, east and west, together with a special one for Speyside, can be useful in illustrating particular characteristics.

The north Highland malts can be said to stretch from the area around Inverness up the east coast to Wick. The whiskies from this area are generally smooth, and while ranging from dry to fruity sweet, are not normally quite as peaty as some of

their more southerly neighbours. Whisky from the
southern Highlands – gen-
erally speaking, around the
Perthshire area and to the
west – is, as might be
expected, softer and lighter
in character, often reasonably sweet but with one or
two dry examples. The
western Highlands is the
smallest of the Highland
sub-divisions, encompass-
ing the area from Oban to
Fort William with their
smooth, rounded whiskies.
The eastern Highlands has
distilleries spread out along

the North Sea coast from Brechin in the south to Banff in the
north. The whiskies in this area offer a wide range of styles,
one of the widest of any of the sub-divisions, from fruity
sweetness to peaty dryness.

The largest and most famous of the Highland sub-divisions
is that of **Speyside**, producing a range of single malts whose
names are instantly recognizable, even to non-whisky
drinkers: Macallan, Glenfiddich, Glenfarclas and Glenlivet.
The area is concentrated around the Elgin–Dufftown district,
a picturesque and fertile area whose remoteness made it an
ideal location for the whisky smugglers of past centuries to

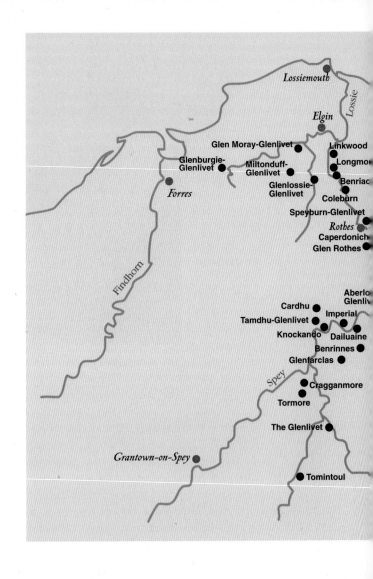

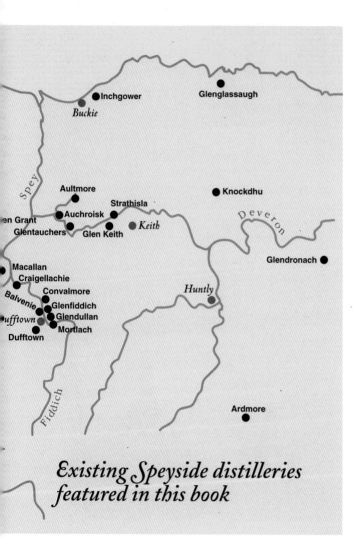

Existing Speyside distilleries featured in this book

escape the efforts of the excisemen. Speyside whiskies are recognized as being mellow, with a malty sweetness and light notes of peat: beyond this basic generalization, however, lies a wealth of variety and subtlety, and the Speyside malts can range from the aromatic and flowery to the robust and sherried. Whiskies can be found in this area to satisfy all palates, from the novice to the connoisseur, and for all occasions.

The final Highland sub-group is that of the **Island** whiskies. As might be expected when these are viewed on a map, the classification is not so much based on characteristics as convenience – this is a suitable sub-group in which to deal with the remaining whiskies which do not fit in any other.

At present, the islands concerned are Jura, Mull and Skye in the west, and Orkney in the north. (It does not, of course, include Islay, whose distinctive style merits a category of its own.) However, in 1995 the Isle of Arran was added to this list with the opening of the first legal distillery on the island for 160 years at Lochranza; the single malt produced here should be available early in the new century. Once again, generalizations are difficult to make, with characters ranging from reasonably dry to full, sweet and malty.

As with any classification, these listings should not be taken as hard and fast rules – taste and preferences vary so greatly that they can only be general guidelines. The best way to decide how well particular whiskies fit their supposed regional listing or characteristic is simply to try each one for yourself!

Visiting Scotch Distilleries and Producers

*W*ith more than 250,000 people visiting Scotland's distilleries every year, catering for visitors has become an important means of promotion and source of revenue for the more famous whisky-makers. Many distilleries are happy to accept visitors, and facilities range from a friendly, impromptu guided tour to a high-tech reception centre with organized tour and gift shop.

Once you have decided which distilleries you would like to visit, you can telephone in advance to find out the particular facilities they offer – the telephone numbers of those distilleries which are equipped to receive visitors are given under their entries throughout the book. It is particularly advisable to telephone if you plan to visit during July and August. Although this is the height of the tourist season, it is also the traditional 'silent' period for this industry which was so closely associated with farming: closing the distillery at this time meant that the workers could help to gather in the harvest. The Scotch Whisky Association (tel: [Edinburgh] 0131-229 4383; [London] 0171-629 4384) publishes a useful leaflet detailing over forty distilleries which welcome visitors, together with opening times and booking information. The Scotch Whisky Heritage Centre (tel: 0131-220 0441) and the Scottish Tourist Board (head office, tel: 0131-332 2433) are also useful sources of information.

If you are in Edinburgh, a visit to the Scotch Whisky

The Pagoda Room Restaurant, part of the award-winning Glenturret Visitor Centre at Crieff in Perthshire (Glenturret Distillery Ltd)

Heritage Centre on Castlehill is always a good starting point if you want to find out more about the industry, with exhibits which are both fun and educational. You can travel back through the industry's past, including the days of illicit distillation, viewing all from the comfort of your own motorized whisky cask!

Finally, for the opportunity to see a perfectly preserved traditional distillery, Dallas Dhu at Forres should not be missed if you are travelling through the north east. Established at the end of the nineteenth century, it stands in lovely countryside to the south of the town. It was previously owned by the Distillers Company, who closed it in 1983, and is now operated by the Historic Buildings and Monuments

Commission for Scotland. Although it no longer produces whisky, it offers one of the most interesting distillery visits in Scotland. (Visitors are welcome 1000-1900 1 Apr.–30 Sept. Tel: 01309-72802 for details.)

Towser, the late distillery mouse catcher at Glenturret Distillery. In a career spanning 24 years, Towser caught 28,899 mice, a feat which earned her an entry in the Guinness Book of Records. *She died in 1987 and was succeeded by a new distillery cat, Amber (Glenturret Distillery Ltd)*

Professional Bodies, Merchants and Trade Associations

*A*s explained on pp. 32–33, single malts bottled by the distilleries are generally a marrying of casks from several distillations, with water being added to reduce the whisky to an agreed alcohol by volume strength for bottling. The whisky will also generally undergo a process of cold-temperature filtration to remove the residues which naturally precipitate cloudiness in the drink after dilution, when it is kept at low temperatures, or when it has ice added. Views differ as to whether this alters the character and taste of the whisky: the producers cite scientific evidence to show that there is no alteration to the whisky's character if it is not diluted below 40% alcohol by volume. However, various independent bodies believe that it does, and they offer consumers the chance to test for themselves.

The Scotch Malt Whisky Society (tel: 0131-554 3452) is one of these bodies. It buys from the distilleries selected single malts which it bottles straight from the cask and offers to its members, of whom there are over 18,000 around the world. The society aims to promote the increased understanding, appreciation and discerning consumption of malt whisky and has recently begun day-long whisky schools comprising practicals, lectures and tastings.

The independent spirit merchants, William Cadenhead Ltd (tel: 01586-554258), also subscribe to this view of the chill-filtration process, and pride themselves on maintaining the individuality of each batch of whisky, bottling straight from the cask at cask strength. The company's approach, of minimal interference with the whisky, relatively simple packaging, and the taking of care over content rather than presentation, is designed to appeal to the slightly more experienced whisky drinker. Much of Cadenhead's stock comes from distilleries whose produce is not otherwise available to the public.

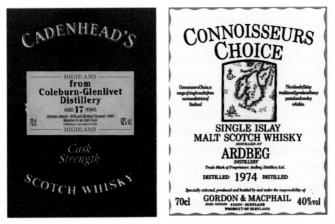

The distinctive labels of independent bottlers, William Cadenhead (left) and Gordon and MacPhail (right)

Gordon and MacPhail of Elgin (tel: 01343-545111) also offer a wide range of their own bottlings from many distilleries. The company, owned and run by the Urquhart family, was established in 1895 as a wine and spirit merchant and licensed grocers, and now is regarded as the world's leading malt whisky specialists. Gordon and MacPhail's policy has always been to buy new whisky direct from a distillery, often in their own casks, warehousing it themselves and bottling it when they consider it to be at its best. Each barrel is assessed for quality, style and quantity available prior to bottling, thereby achieving a consistency and quality of malt for which the company is recognized. As well as single and vatted malts, cask-strength bottlings and unusual blends, they have a large selection of old and rare whiskies.

A relative newcomer to the independent merchants' ranks is the Signatory Vintage Scotch Whisky Company, based in Edinburgh (tel: 0131-555 4988). Founded in the late 1980s, they acquire casks of exceptional age and quality and bottle either diluted to 40%, 43% or 46%, or at cask strength. No colourant is used in their bottlings and only the diluted range is chill-filtered to remove oiliness. There is a variation between bottlings as the number of casks vatted varies.

For those whose interest is in the packaging as much as the contents, the Mini Bottle Club is the world's premier club for collectors of miniatures. Details can be obtained from the membership secretary, c/o 47 Burradon Rd, Burradon, Northumberland NE23 7NF (enclose a s.a.e.).

Finally, if you would like to know more about any aspect of Scotch whisky, the Scotch Whisky Association will happily supply information for you. The association promotes the interests of the Scotch whisky industry in Britain and around the world, and its membership comprises almost all companies involved in the industry. The Public Affairs office is in London (tel: 0171-629 4384), while the head office is in Edinburgh (tel: 0131-229 4383).

Reading the Label

The label on a whisky bottle will allow you to identify a few basic facts about its contents even before you open the bottle – most obviously, the brand and its producers, the type of whisky it is, and its age, quantity and strength. Single malts normally proclaim themselves as such, and the identification of the producing distillery acts as a double check. A label which states a bottle's contents to be malt, but without the words 'single' or 'unblended', is probably vatted. Grains and blends likewise will identify themselves, and while most de luxe whiskies will also do so, this is not always the case. Blends of all kinds will carry the name of the blenders rather than of any distillery.

Where whiskies carry an age statement on the label, this will be the age of the youngest whisky in the bottle. Instead of this, some malts may give the year of their distillation. Single malts are usually eight years old and upwards, becoming more expensive as their age increases. It is generally held, however, that up to fifteen years is a good maturation period for whisky, and while some whiskies improve by maturing beyond this period, not all do of necessity – it depends on the individual whisky. Whiskies for general consumption in the UK are normally packaged in 70 or 75 cl bottles, but you may also come upon 1 litre bottles.

Most whiskies are sold at 40% alcohol by volume. The system for measuring spirit strength in Britain changed in

brand name

type of whisky

The **GLENLIVET**
12
A G E D   YEARS

age of whisky

Pure Single Malt Scotch Whisky

P R O D U C T   O F   S C O T L A N D

"UNHURRIED SINCE 1824"
An exceptional whisky from The Glenlivet Distillery, aged in oak casks for more than twelve unhurried years
Distilled in Scotland by
GEORGE & J. G. SMITH
THE GLENLIVET DISTILLERY · AB37 9DD
BOTTLED IN SCOTLAND

70 cl.e   40%vol.

distiller

bottle volume   strength (alcohol by volume)

VATTED MALT   BLEND   DE LUXE

YEARS **12** OLD
PRIDE of ISLAY
Malt
SCOTCH WHISKY
PRODUCED ON THE ISLE OF ISLAY
GORDON & MACPHAIL
ELGIN, SCOTLAND
70d   40%vol

CUTTY SARK
BLENDED
SCOTS WHISKY
100% Scotch Whiskies
from Scotland's best Distilleries
BERRY BROS & RUDD Lⁿ
3, ST JAMES'S STREET, LONDON
40% vol.   c 700 ml
Product of Scotland
Distilled, Blended and Bottled in Scotland

ISLAY MIST
75d   40% Vol
Deluxe
BLENDED SCOTCH WHISKY
DISTILLED BLENDED AND BOTTLED IN SCOTLAND

The component parts of a single malt whisky label (top), together with examples of labels from other types of whisky

53

1980 from the older and more complicated Sikes system of measuring proof strength, to the Organization of Legal Metrology, or OIML system, which measures spirit strength as a percentage of volume at 20 °C. Whisky is distilled at a much higher content than its final form for consumption. Water may be added before it goes into the cask, to bring it down to 68.5% alcohol by volume, a standard measure. Some evaporation takes place as the whisky matures, leaving a final cask strength of around 45–60%. Cask-strength whiskies are available, but most single malts have to have water added to bring them down to 40% or 43% (normally for the export market) strength for bottling. However, the industry may move towards a standard strength of 40% after a 1988 European Community directive which based the amount of duty on the alcoholic strength of a spirit. 40% alcohol by volume is equivalent to the old measure of 70° proof and, confusingly, 80° proof in the USA, which uses a slightly different system again.

The
Whiskies
of
Scotland

Taste Rating

The discussions on the different whiskies which follow contain a taste rating of 1–5. This is not intended to be a judgement on the quality or relative standard of the spirit, nor is it possible to place strength and flavour together satisfactorily. Rather, it can be used as an indicator of accessibility of the whisky for a relatively inexperienced palate. A whisky may be mild or strong and still either lack flavour or exude it, so this rating concerns the degree of flavour, while at the same time allowing for the strength interfering with a person's ability to appreciate the flavour. The basic categories are as follows:

1   Popular with particular palates; spirituous, with a very mild flavour

2   Good for beginners; appealing taste and flavour for most palates at certain times

2–3   Also good for beginners, but a little stronger than **2**. One to return to again and again

3   A dram for everyone; not too powerful, with pleasant sensations

3–4   This should also appeal to most tastes, but is slightly stronger, so the palate requires a little more experience

4   Very pleasing; a stronger spirit, ideal for those with more experience

5   Robust; only for the well developed palate

HIGHLAND
SINGLE MALT
SCOTCH WHISKY

ABERFELDY

distillery was established in 1898 on the *road* to *Perth* and south *side* of the *RIVER TAY*. Fresh *spring water* is taken from the nearby *PITILIE burn* and used to produce this *UNIQUE single MALT* ℀ *SCOTCH WHISKY* with its *distinctive PEATY* nose.

AGED **15** YEARS

Distilled & Bottled in SCOTLAND
ABERFELDY DISTILLERY
Aberfeldy, Perthshire, Scotland.

43% vol 70 cl

Aberfeldy

Aberfeldy Distillery,
Aberfeldy, Perthshire

TYPE	
Single malt	
BOTTLING AGE	
15 years	
STRENGTH	
43%	
TASTE RATING	
3	
MINIATURES	
Yes	

COMMENTS

Basically a dry malt with a medium body and clean, fresh character, but with a distinctly peaty background.

VISITORS

Visitors are welcome 0930–1630 Mon.–Fri. (times are restricted in winter). Telephone 01887-820330.

*A*berfeldy Distillery stands near the River Tay, at the town from which it takes its name. Building began in 1896 and the distillery opened two years later. It was built by Dewar but passed with that company into the ownership of the Distillers Company Ltd in 1925. Almost all of its production now goes into United Distillers' blends, most notably Dewar's White Label. The single malt is still relatively rare, only becoming available in official bottlings in the Distillery (Flora and Fauna) Malts series early in the 1990s.

Aberlour

Aberlour-Glenlivet Distillery,
Aberlour, Banffshire

TYPE
Single malt

BOTTLING AGE
10, 12 years

STRENGTH
40%, 43%

TASTE RATING
3

MINIATURES
Yes

COMMENTS
A smooth, rich, sherried Spey-side malt which is an ideal after-dinner drink.

VISITORS
Visitors are welcome by appointment. Telephone 01340-8714204 to arrange.

*E*stablished in the 1860s, Aberlour Distillery was rebuilt in the early 1880s after its destruction in a fire. It sits below Ben Rinnes from whose slopes it draws its water, said to be an important characteristic of its distinctive flavour. In the distillery grounds is the well of St Drostan (or Dunstan), the tenth-century missionary and patron saint of Aberlour who later became Archbishop of Canterbury. Since its acquisition by the Pernod Ricard company in 1974, Aberlour has been well marketed in France, where it is one of the most popular of Scotch whiskies. The company also owns the Irish Distillers Group.

An
CNOC
SINGLE HIGHLAND MALT
SCOTCH WHISKY

12
YEARS OLD

DISTILLED AND MATURED IN SCOTLAND BY
THE KNOCKDHU DISTILLERY CO, BANFFSHIRE
BOTTLED IN SCOTLAND

Produce of Scotland

An Cnoc

*Knockdhu Distillery,
Knock, Banffshire*

TYPE
Single malt

BOTTLING AGE
12 years

STRENGTH
40%

TASTE RATING
2–3

MINIATURES
Yes

COMMENTS
An Cnoc's dryish aroma is complemented by a mellow sweetness in the flavour. This Highland malt was previously known as Knockdhu.

VISITORS
The distillery is not open to visitors.

Knockdhu Distillery was established in 1893 on a favoured site: with water available from Knock Hill, barley from the nearby farmlands, and a good supply of local peat. Although both its buildings and machinery have since been modified, the production process remains essentially the same, with the two originally designed pot stills remaining. Previously owned by the Distillers Company Ltd and licensed to Haig, Knockdhu was sold in 1988 to Inver House Distillers, who reopened it after a lengthy silent period. Its single malt is one of the few which does not take its distillery's name.

The
Antiquary

United Distillers,
Kilmarnock, Ayrshire

TYPE
De luxe blend

BOTTLING AGE
12 years

STRENGTH
40%

TASTE RATING
3

MINIATURES
Yes

COMMENTS
A smooth, well-balanced, premium blend which displays the mellowness expected from its blend of whiskies all aged 12 years and over.

Now owned by United Distillers, Sanderson is the producer of The Antiquary. The company was one of the blenders who began trading in the early–to–mid nineteenth century, who were responsible for the popularizing of blended whiskies in the lucrative markets of southern England. Sanderson was also a founder of the North British Distillery company in 1885, ensuring supplies of good grain whisky for his blends.

CONNOISSEURS CHOICE

Connoisseurs Choice, range of single malt from various distincts of Scotland

The ideal of fatty traditional of greedos delicacy pointed and smokey whiskies

SINGLE ISLAY
MALT SCOTCH WHISKY
BOTTLED AT
ARDBEG
DISTILLERY
Trade Mark of Proprietors Ardbeg Distillery Ltd.

DISTILLED **1974** DISTILLED

Specially selected, produced and bottled by and under the responsibility of

70cl **GORDON & MACPHAIL** 40%vol
ELGIN, SCOTLAND
PRODUCT OF SCOTLAND

Ardbeg
Ardbeg Distillery,
Port Ellen, Islay, Argyllshire

TYPE
Single malt

BOTTLING AGE
Varies

STRENGTH
Varies

TASTE RATING
5

MINIATURES
Yes

COMMENTS
With a dominant aroma and insistent peatiness, Ardbeg's flavour is balanced by sweeter tones. Considered the most pungent of all Scotch whiskies, it is available from independent bottlers.

VISITORS
The distillery is not suitable for visitors.

*T*his distillery was opened in 1815, and was one of several established near the sea in an area which was originally used by smugglers. It was bought by Hiram Walker in the 1950s, primarily to use its produce in blending; blenders use Islay malts in the way that a chef might use a strong flavour like garlic. Nearby Lochs Uigeadale and Arinambeast supply the water which, together with local peat, produces a distinctively Islay malt. Ardbeg is operated by Allied Distillers but they do not sell its produce officially as a single malt.

Ardmore

Ardmore Distillery,
Kennethmont, Aberdeenshire

TYPE
Single malt

BOTTLING AGE
Varies

STRENGTH
Varies

TASTE RATING
4

MINIATURES
Yes

COMMENTS
A full-bodied Speyside malt which is both robust and sweet. An ideal after-dinner dram, although it is not easy to come by; available as a single malt only through independent bottlers.

VISITORS
Visitors are welcome by appointment. Telephone 01464-3213 to arrange.

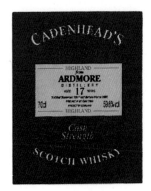

The distillery at Ardmore was built in 1898 by the Teacher family of whisky merchants and blenders. Since that time almost all its production has gone into Teacher's blends, most famously Highland Cream. Today it is operated by Allied Distillers, so its product also features prominently in Allied's other blends. Although the distillery has been modernized it still retains some of the original equipment, such as coal-fired stills, which were used in the production of whisky at the end of the nineteenth century.

Auchentoshan

Auchentoshan Distillery,
Dalmuir, Dunbartonshire

TYPE
Single malt

BOTTLING AGE
Select, 10, 21 years

STRENGTH
40%, 43%

TASTE RATING
2–3

MINIATURES
Yes

COMMENTS
A light, sweetish whisky whose smooth qualities are perhaps partially owed to the process of triple, rather than the more common double distillation.

VISITORS
The distillery is not open to visitors.

Although Auchentoshan Distillery lies south of the Highland Line (the line initiated by the Customs and Excise to differentiate area boundaries between styles of whisky), it uses water from north of the line, so theoretically could be said to have a foot in both camps. It is, however, officially recognized as a Lowland distillery and whisky. Founded in the early nineteenth century, part of its interesting history includes surviving bombing in the Clydebank Blitz during the Second World War, when a stream of blazing whisky was said to have flowed from the building. It is presently owned by Morrison Bowmore, also owners of Bowmore and Glen Garioch distilleries.

Aultmore

Aultmore Distillery,
Aultmore, Keith, Banffshire

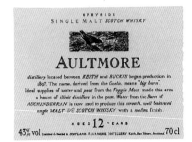

TYPE
Single malt

BOTTLING AGE
12 years

STRENGTH
43%

TASTE RATING
3

MINIATURES
Yes

COMMENTS
A faintly peaty aroma leads into this smooth, fruity, well-balanced whisky which has become – deservedly – better known in recent years.

VISITORS
The distillery is open to visitors by appointment only. Telephone 01542-882762.

*A*ultmore Distillery was established in 1895 at the tail-end of the whisky boom by the owner of the older Benrinnes Distillery. The area, with its abundant peat and water supplies, was infamous in the past for illicit distilling. Peat used in the production process is taken from a nearby moss, and the water is taken from local springs. The distillery passed to Dewars in 1923, and was improved and upgraded in the 1970s. It is now owned by United Distillers who have been officially bottling its single malt in their Distillery (Flora and Fauna) Malts series since the early 1990s.

THE BAILIE NICOL JARVIE
→ BLEND OF ←
Old Scotch Whisky

PRODUCE OF SCOTLAND

Sole Proprietors

NICOL ANDERSON & Cº LTº

QUEEN'S DOCK

VERY OLD RESERVE   LEITH

The Bailie Nicol Jarvie

MacDonald and Muir,
Leith, Edinburgh

TYPE
Blend

BOTTLING AGE
12 years

STRENGTH
40%

TASTE RATING
2

MINIATURES
Yes

COMMENTS
A light, subtle whisky with a sweet, well-balanced aroma and a smooth, lingering finish.

*F*ounded in 1893 in Leith by Roderick Macdonald and Alexander Muir, Macdonald and Muir Ltd is one of the few remaining independent family-owned and -controlled companies left in the Scotch whisky trade. 'The Bailie', or 'BNJ' as it is also known, is named after the fictional magistrate in Walter Scott's *Rob Roy*. Although a popular brand in the early years of this century (particularly in military circles), in recent years production had been severely limited. However, the brand was relaunched in October 1994 and production stepped up following a change in the blend receipe.

Balblair

Balblair Distillery,
Edderton, Tain, Ross-shire

TYPE
Single malt

BOTTLING AGE
10 years

STRENGTH
40%

TASTE RATING
3

MINIATURES
Yes

COMMENTS
A distinctive Highland malt whose slightly dry sharpness is nicely balanced by a light note of sweetness. Good as an aperitif, it is available from independent bottlers.

VISITORS
The distillery has no reception centre, but visitors are welcome by appointment. Telephone 01862-821273.

Although its origins are lost in the mists of illicit distillation, it is claimed that Balblair was founded in 1749, which would make it one of the oldest distilleries in the country. The present buildings, dating from the 1870s, are set in pretty countryside in an area known as the 'parish of peats'. The distillery had very recently been mothballed by its then owners, Allied Distillers, but was acquired from them in the spring of 1996 by the independent Inver House Distillers. The addition of Balblair gives Inver House four malt distilleries – Knockdhu, Speyburn-Glenlivet and Pultney, the latter also a recent purchase from Allied.

Ballantine's Finest

*Allied Distillers,
Dumbarton, Dunbartonshire*

TYPE
Blend

BOTTLING AGE
40%, 43%

STRENGTH
2–3

MINIATURES
Yes

COMMENTS
Ballantine's Finest is, like Allied Distillers' other blends, characteristically mellow and well-rounded with a soft, un-assertive peaty flavour. Their range of blends also includes Ballantine's Gold Seal (12 years old), Ballantine's 17 Years Old and Ballantine's 30-year-old, considered to be one of the oldest (and also one of the most expensive) blends available.

VISITORS
The plant is not suitable for visitors.

*B*allantine's was bought in 1936 by Hiram Walker as one of their first moves into the Scotch whisky market. Glenburgie and Miltonduff distilleries followed in 1937 and their new, giant complex in Dumbarton, featuring grain and malt distilleries, was operational the following year. Today the group is owned by Allied Domecq and operated by their wholly Scottish-based subsidiary, Allied Distillers. The Dumbarton plant is renowned locally for its 'Scotchwatch' alarm system, comprising 100-odd noisy Chinese geese!

Balmenach

*Balmenach Distillery,
Cromdale, Moray*

TYPE

Single malt

BOTTLING AGE

12 years

STRENGTH

43%

TASTE RATING

4

MINIATURES

Yes

COMMENTS

A complicated, full-bodied malt best suited as an after-dinner dram.

SPEYSIDE
SINGLE MALT
SCOTCH WHISKY

Sometime in the early 19th, after walking in the CROMDALE hills with his 2 BROTHERS, James McGregor settled and established

BALMENACH

distillery. Spring water from beneath those same HILLS is still used to produce this RICH flavoured single MALT SCOTCH WHISKY of exemplary quality.

AGED 12 YEARS

43% vol   Distilled & Bottled in SCOTLAND   70cl
BALMENACH DISTILLERY, Cromdale, Moray, Scotland

*T*he Balmenach Distillery, in the Haughs of Cromdale, is set in an area which was notorious for illicit distilling for many years before the Licensing Act of 1823. Built in 1824 by James McGregor (great-grandfather of Sir Robert Bruce Lockhart, author of the classic 1951 book, *Scotch*), Balmenach was one of the first distilleries in the Highlands to be licensed under the 1823 act. The distillery was acquired by United Distillers and most of its production went into the company's blends but has since been closed. The single malt is still relatively rare, only becoming available in official bottlings in the Distillery (Flora and Fauna) Malts series early in the 1990s.

SINGLE MALT

ESTᵈ 1892

Distilled at

THE BALVENIE

Distillery, Banffshire
SCOTLAND

FOUNDER'S RESERVE
MALT SCOTCH WHISKY

AGED **10** YEARS

The Balvenie Distillery has been owned
AND MANAGED BY OUR INDEPENDENT
family company for five generations.
⬤ AT BALVENIE ⬤
there are four maltmen, three mashmen,
three tun room men, and three stillmen
AND BETWEEN THEM
they make all The Balvenie we bottle.

THE BALVENIE MALTMASTER

THE BALVENIE DISTILLERY COMPANY, BALVENIE MALTINGS, DUFFTOWN,
BANFFSHIRE, SCOTLAND AB55 4BB

70 cl e   PRODUCT OF SCOTLAND   40% vol

The Balvenie

Balvenie Distillery,
Dufftown, Keith, Banffshire

TYPE
Single malt

BOTTLING AGE
10 years (Founder's Reserve),
12 years (Doublewood),
15 years (Single Barrel)

STRENGTH
Varies

TASTE RATING
3–4

MINIATURES
Yes

COMMENTS

Founder's Reserve has a rich colour, bouquet and flavour with a smooth, clean, dry finish. Doublewood is full-bodied, yet smooth and mellow, and Single Barrel, a harder-to-obtain 15-year-old, is a single-cask bottling.

VISITORS

The distillery is not open to visitors.

Built in 1892 near the ruins of fourteenth-century Balvenie Castle by the Grants of Glenfiddich, Balvenie Distillery has now been owned by an independent family company for five generations. Balvenie Distillery still grows its own barley, malts in its own traditional floor maltings, employs coopers to tend the barrels and coppersmiths to tend the stills. The Balvenie is most unusual in producing a range of three malt whiskies of different age and character.

Banff

Banff Distillery,
Banff, Banffshire

TYPE

Single malt

BOTTLING AGE

Varies

STRENGTH

Varies

TASTE RATING

2–3

MINIATURES

Yes

COMMENTS

A pleasant, slightly smoky, sweet bouquet leads into a whisky with a rather assertive taste. A rare malt, available from independent merchants only.

*T*his distillery had an eventful history after its founding in 1863. It survived damage by fire in the 1870s, and was one of the few distilleries to be bombed during the Second World War, when thousands of gallons of whisky had to be thrown away to prevent the spread of fire. It was reported that the whisky running over the land and into nearby streams caused intoxication among the local farm animals and birds, and that dairy cows could not stand up to be milked! The distillery also once supplied whisky to Parliament. It was closed down by its parent company, the Distillers Company Ltd, in 1983, and has since been demolished.

Bell's Extra Special

United Distillers, Glasgow

TYPE
Blend

BOTTLING AGE
40%

STRENGTH
2–3

TASTE RATING
Yes

COMMENTS

The most popular blend in the UK, Bell's Extra Special is a pleasant, medium-bodied whisky with a nutty aroma and a spicy flavour.

*T*he merchants and blending company which ultimately became Arthur Bell & Sons was begun in Perth in 1825. Bell himself joined the firm as a traveller in the 1840s and became a partner in 1851. The 'Extra Special' name, accompanied by Bell's signature, was registered as a trade mark in 1895. Large-scale expansion came in the 1930s after the ending of Prohibition in the USA, when Bell acquired three of the company's subsequent complement of five distilleries. Bell's is now owned by United Distillers who relaunched Bell's Extra Special as an 8-year-old blend in 1994.

Ben Nevis

Ben Nevis Distillery,
Fort William, Inverness-shire

TYPE
Single malt

BOTTLING AGE
19, 25, 26 years

STRENGTH
Varies

TASTE RATING
3

MINIATURES
No

COMMENTS
Ranging from pale amber to a deep, golden colour, Ben Nevis is characterized by its fresh, slightly peaty flavour and smooth finish.

VISITORS
Visitors are welcome 0900–1700 Mon.–Fri. all year (0900–1730 Jul.–Aug.) and 1000–1600 Sat., Easter–Sep. Larger parties are advised to telephone 01397-700200 to arrange.

*B*en Nevis Distillery, standing at the foot of Scotland's highest mountain, is one of the oldest distilleries in Scotland. It was founded at Fort William by the famous local character, 'Long' John Macdonald in 1825. (The brand name of Long John and the distillery company became separated.) After more than 100 years and three generations in the family, the distillery was sold in 1941. The subsiquent addition of a patent still made the distillery one of the few that could produce both malt and grain under one roof , and it received a new lease of life in the 1980s following its acquisition by the Nikka Whisky Distilling Co. of Japan.

BENRIACH DISTILLERY
EST. 1898
A SINGLE
PURE HIGHLAND MALT
Scotch Whisky
Benriach Distillery, in the heart of the Highlands,
still malts its own barley. The resulting whisky has
a unique and attractive delicacy
PRODUCED AND BOTTLED BY THE
BENRIACH
DISTILLERY C?
ELGIN, MORAYSHIRE, SCOTLAND, IV30 3SJ
Distilled and Bottled in Scotland
AGED 10 YEARS
70 cl ℮ 43%vol

Benriach

*Benriach Distillery,
Elgin, Moray*

TYPE
Single malt

BOTTLING AGE
10 years

STRENGTH
43%

TASTE RATING
4

MINIATURES
Yes

COMMENTS
A medium-bodied, fruity whisky with sweetish overtones and a gently malty finish. A new bottling has been available from the distillery since 1994.

VISITORS
The distillery is not open to visitors.

Originally built in the 1890s, Benriach was closed in 1900, after recession hit the previously booming whisky industry. It was refitted and reopened in 1965, although not completely modernized, still retaining its hand-turned malting floor. The company is owned by Seagram, and most of its produce goes into their blends. Although the distillery now produces its own, official bottling, this is still not an easy whisky to come across.

Benrinnes

*Benrinnes Distillery,
Aberlour, Banffshire*

TYPE
Single malt

BOTTLING AGE
15 years

STRENGTH
43%

TASTE RATING
4

MINIATURES
Yes

COMMENTS
This is a complex Speyside malt which has hints of wood and grass to its flavour, and a fruity aftertaste.

VISITORS
The distillery is open to visitors by appointment only. Telephone 01340-871215.

*B*uilt almost 700 feet up the slopes of Ben Rinnes, from which it takes its name, this distillery is believed to have been founded in 1835 although evidence exists of distilling on this site in 1826. It was largely rebuilt and modernized in the 1950s. Most of its production is distilled three times rather than the more usual twice, and almost all is used in United Distillers' blends. The single malt is still relatively rare, only becoming available in official bottlings in the Distillery (Flora and Fauna) Malts series early in the 1990s.

Benromach

*Benromach Distillery,
Forres, Moray*

TYPE
Single malt

BOTTLING AGE
Varies

STRENGTH
Varies

TASTE RATING
2–3

MINIATURES
Yes

COMMENTS
Subtle and sweet, this Speyside malt has a gentle, fragrant palate and refreshing aftertaste. It is available from independent merchants.

*B*enromach was built just outside Forres in 1898, in the years of expansion for the whisky industry, and it underwent extensive reconstruction in 1966 and 1974. It passed through several hands until coming to rest with the Distillers Company Ltd in 1953. Supplies of the whisky may not be easy to come by for the immediate future, as the distillery was closed from 1983 to 1993, when it was sold by United Distillers to the independent merchants and bottlers Gordon and MacPhail. Since then it has been re-fitted, with a first new distillation set to take place in 1996.

Big "T"

*Tomatin Distillery Company,
Tomatin, Inverness-shire*

TYPE
Blend and de luxe
5 years (standard blend)

BOTTLING AGE
12 years (de luxe)

STRENGTH
40%, 43%

TASTE RATING
1 (standard blend)
2 (de luxe)

MINIATURES
Yes; de luxe and standard

COMMENTS
Big "T" standard blend is a whisky of light-to-medium body with a fresh, malty sweetness, well-balanced by a hint of peat. The 12-year-old de luxe is an extremely smooth blend, most of which is reserved for export.

VISITORS
Visitors can visit the malt whisky distillery; see the entry on Tomatin for details.

FINEST SCOTCH WHISKY

BIG "T"
SCOTCH WHISKY
100% BLENDED SCOTCH WHISKIES
BLENDED AND BOTTLED
IN SCOTLAND BY
THE TOMATIN DISTILLERY COMPANY LTD.
TOMATIN SCOTLAND

43% Vol   75 cl

The Tomatin Distillery Company's premises is not only one of the highest in the country (at over 1000 feet up in the Monadhliath Mountains), it is also the largest-capacity distillery in the country, with production as high as five million gallons per annum. The company declined in the 1980s and went into receivership, but was bought by the Japanese firms of Takara Schuzo and Okura, thus becoming the first Scotch whisky distillery to be acquired by Japanese owners.

United Distillers, Banbeath, Leven, Fife

TYPE
Blend

STRENGTH
40%

TASTE RATING
2

MINIATURES
Yes

COMMENTS
A clean, pleasantly mild blend, Black & White has a fresh, grassy flavour, which is complemented by a light sweetness.

*B*lack & White is the standard blend of the company begun in 1884 by James Buchanan as a whisky blenders and merchants in London. Within a year it was a success, with a contract to supply the House of Commons, and the firm was one of the prime movers in the introduction of blended whiskies to the English market. The whisky was bottled and labelled in a very distinctive black and white livery, and this popular nickname eventually was adopted as the brand name. The company amalgamated with Dewar's in 1915, and both joined the Distillers Company ten years later. Black & White is currently available only outside the UK.

Black Bottle

Allied Distillers,
Dumbarton, Dunbartonshire

TYPE
Blend

STRENGTH
40%

TASTE RATING
2–3

MINIATURES
Yes

COMMENTS
Black Bottle is a smooth, superior-quality blend with a fresh hint of peat, complemented by sweeter, malty notes.

VISITORS
The plant is not suitable for visitors.

*B*lack Bottle was first produced by a family of merchants from Aberdeen in 1879, and has been a premium blend ever since it first appeared on the market. The company was sold to Long John International in 1959, later being acquired by Allied Distillers in 1990, before ultimately passing into the control of Matthew Gloag, the producers of The Famous Grouse blend. A big seller in the Scottish market, Black Bottle is linked to Laphroaig. Its distinctive pot-still-shaped bottle, used almost since its first appearance, rapidly became its trademark and has remained virtually unchanged to the present day.

LOWLAND
SINGLE MALT
SCOTCH WHISKY

The *Broad Leaved Helleborine*,
a rare species of *wild orchid*, can be found growing
in the *ancient oak woodland* behind the

BLADNOCH

distillery. The most southerly in *SCOTLAND*,
founded in the *early* 1800's, & the
distillery stands by the *RIVER BLADNOCH*
near *Wigtown*. It produces a *distinctive*
LOWLAND single MALT WHISKY – delicate and
fruity with a *lemony* aroma and *taste*.

AGED **10** YEARS

43% vol   70 cl

Distilled & Bottled in *SCOTLAND*
BLADNOCH DISTILLERY, Bladnoch, Wigtownshire, Scotland

Bladnoch

Bladnoch Distillery, Bladnoch,
Wigtown, Wigtownshire

TYPE
Single malt

BOTTLING AGE
10 years

STRENGTH
43%

TASTE RATING
3

MINIATURES
Yes

COMMENTS
Bladnoch is a light-to-medium-bodied malt with a light, fragrant, lemony aroma and a gentle, unassertive flavour with fruity tones.

*B*ladnoch was Scotland's most southerly distillery, in Wigtownshire, and was also one of its oldest. It was built in 1817 and stood on the banks of the River Bladnoch, in the village of the same name. It had many owners throughout the course of the twentieth century, the latest being United Distillers. The distillery is now closed. Bladnoch's single malt is still relatively rare, only becoming available in official bottlings in UD's Distillery (Flora and Fauna) Malts series early in the 1990s.

Blair Athol

*Blair Athol Distillery,
Pitlochry, Perthshire*

TYPE

Single malt

BOTTLING AGE

12 years

STRENGTH

43%

TASTE RATING

2–3

MINIATURES

Yes

COMMENTS

Blair Athol is a light, fresh single malt with dry notes and a hint of smokiness.

VISITORS

Visitors are welcome 0930–1700 Mon.-Sat. all year, and 1200–1700 Sun., Easter–October. Telephone 01796-472234 to arrange.

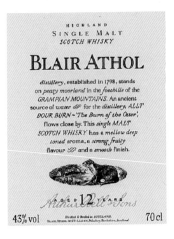

*T*his is a picturesquely sited distillery on a wooded hillside on the outskirts of the pretty Perthshire tourist centre of Pitlochry. Blair Athol is unusual in that it is twelve miles distant from the village after which it is named. Established in 1825, the distillery was bought by Bell in 1933 and sympathetically upgraded. It is now owned by United Distillers. Its water comes from the Allt Dour (Burn of the Otter) which flows past the distillery en route to the River Tummel.

Bowmore

Bowmore Distillery,
Bowmore, Islay, Argyllshire

TYPE
Single malt

BOTTLING AGE
Legend, 12, 17, 21,
22, 25, 30 years

STRENGTH
40%, 43%

TASTE RATING
3

MINIATURES
Yes

COMMENTS

With its pleasant aroma and peaty–fruity flavour, Bowmore is a good Islay malt for newcomers to these distinctive whiskies to try.

VISITORS

Visitors are welcome by appointment. Telephone 01496-810671 to arrange.

*E*stablished in the 1770s, Bowmore is reputed to be the oldest legal distillery on Islay. It stands in the island's main town and overlooks Loch Indaal, and its water is taken from the peaty River Laggan. The distillery has passed through several hands in the twentieth century, but it has been a consistently thriving concern since its acquisition in 1963 by Stanley P. Morrison of Glasgow. The company is now Morrison Bowmore, and this is their flagship distillery.

Bruichladdich

Bruichladdich Distillery,
Bruichladdich, Islay,
Argyllshire

TYPE
Single malt

BOTTLING AGE
10, 15, 21 years

STRENGTH
40%

TASTE RATING
3

MINIATURES
Yes

COMMENTS
A subtle malt, and less medicinal in its flavour than other Islay whiskies, Bruichladdich is a lightish, dry, fresh-tasting whisky.

*B*uilt in 1881, Bruichladdich is Scotland's most westerly distillery. Its water comes from an inland reservoir and, unlike the other distilleries, is not drawn from springs which have flowed over peaty land; this has been suggested as a reason why its peaty flavour is less intense than other Islay malts. Bruichladdich was owned by Invergordon Distillers from 1972 until 1993, but since the company's acquisition that year by Whyte & Mackay, it has been mothballed along with two of the group's other distilleries, Tamnavulin and Tullibardine.

Bunnahabhain

Bunnahabhain Distillery,
Port Askaig, Islay, Argyllshire

TYPE	Single malt
BOTTLING AGE	12 years
STRENGTH	40%
TASTE RATING	3
MINIATURES	Yes

COMMENTS

Less characteristically peaty than some other Islay malts, Bunnahabhain is a mellow whisky with an aromatic flavour.

VISITORS

Visitors are welcome by appointment. Telephone 01496-840646 to arrange.

 $\mathcal{B}$ unnahabhain, on the north shore of Islay, is one of the more isolated of the island's distilleries. Founded in 1881, it has changed very little in the intervening century despite expansion in the 1960s. All its production formerly went into blends. Bunnahabhain was owned by the Islay Distillery Company who bought Glen Rothes Distillery in 1887, together forming the Highland Distilleries Company. They still own Bunnahabhain today.

Cameron Brig

Cameronbridge Distillery,
Cameron Bridge, Fife

TYPE

Grain

STRENGTH

40%

TASTE RATING

1

MINIATURES

Yes

COMMENTS

Like other grain whiskies, a lighter spirit than malt, with a fresh taste and an element of smoothness.

VISITORS

The distillery is not open to visitors.

*C*ameronbridge Distillery had been operating for several years before it was acquired in 1824 by John Haig, one of the famous family of Lowland whisky distillers. One of its most famous directors, who subsequently became a director at the Distillers Company Ltd, was Field Marshal Douglas Haig, commander-in-chief of the British Army on the Western Front during the First World War. Haig's company were among the founders of the Distillers Company in 1877, and United Distillers still own the distillery today. Cameronbridge produced both grain and malt whisky using a mixture of pot and patent stills until 1929 before finally concentrating on grain alone.

Caol Ila

Caol Ila Distillery,
Port Askaig, Islay, Argyllshire

ISLAY
SINGLE MALT *SCOTCH WHISKY*

CAOL ILA

distillery, built in 1846 is situated near *Port Askaig* on the *Isle of Islay.*
Steamers used to call twice a week to collect *whisky* from this remote
site in a cove facing the *Isle of Jura.* Water supplies for mashing
come from *Loch nam Ban* although the sea provides *water for
condensing* Unusual for an *Islay* this *single MALT SCOTCH
WHISKY* has a *fresh aroma* and a *light yet well rounded* flavour.

A G E D **15** Y E A R S

43% VOl Distilled & Bottled in SCOTLAND. CAOL ILA DISTILLERY, Port Askaig, Isle of Islay, Scotland 70 cl

TYPE
Single malt

BOTTLING AGE
15 years

STRENGTH
43%

TASTE RATING
4

MINIATURES
Yes

COMMENTS

Nicely balanced, Caol Ila is not the most peaty of the Islay whiskies, but is pleasantly dry with a well-rounded body.

VISITORS

Visitors are welcome Mon.–Fri. by appointment. Telephone 01496-840207 to arrange.

*C*aol Ila was established in 1846 and overlooks the Sound of Islay (which is also the English translation of its name). It previously used its own wharf for the despatching of its product. The distillery has been rebuilt twice, at almost 100-year intervals, in 1879 and 1972. The most recent modernization almost doubled the distillery's output. Caol Ila is now owned by United Distillers. The single malt is still relatively rare, only becoming available in official bottlings in UD's Distillery (Flora and Fauna) Malts series early in the 1990s.

Caperdonich

Caperdonich Distillery,
Rothes, Moray

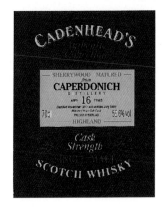

TYPE

Single malt

BOTTLING AGE

Varies

STRENGTH

Varies

TASTE RATING

3

MINIATURES

Yes

COMMENTS

A pleasant Speyside malt of light-to-medium body, with a delicately fruity flavour combined with a hint of peat.

VISITORS

The distillery is not open to visitors.

*O*riginally owned by J & J Grant, this distillery was built across the road from their main production centre at Glen Grant. The two distilleries were to be treated as one for licensing purposes, so a pipe spanned the road to carry the produce of Caperdonich (then known as Glen Grant Number Two) across for blending. Built to take advantage of the boom years of the 1890s, it suffered with the fall-off in consumption and was closed in the early 1900s, waiting over sixty years for renovation and reopening under the new name of Caperdonich. Most of its produce goes into blends, with only some available from independent merchants.

Cardhu

Cardhu Distillery,
Knockando, Moray

TYPE

Single malt

BOTTLING AGE

12 years

STRENGTH

40%

TASTE RATING

2–3

MINIATURES

Yes

COMMENTS

A smooth, light malt of silky character and delicate, sweet flavour which make it accessible to all from the novice to the connoisseur.

VISITORS

Visitors are welcome 0930–1630 Mon.–Fri. all year, and 0930–1630 Sat., May–Sept. Telephone 01340-810204.

*W*hisky distilling had been carried on illegally in this area for a long time before Cardow Distillery, as it was then, was founded and licensed in 1824. The distillery was bought by John Walker of Kilmarnock during the boom years of the 1890s, producing a vatted and a single malt under the Cardhu name. It was modernized in 1965 and its single malt was relaunched, with the distillery name being changed in 1981 to match that of its product. It is now owned by United Distillers. Cardhu enjoys a splendid situation overlooking the Spey valley and has recently been refurbished.

Chivas Regal

Chivas Brothers,
Paisley, Renfrewshire

TYPE

De luxe

BOTTLING AGE

12 years

STRENGTH

40%

TASTE RATING

2–3

MINIATURES

Yes

COMMENTS

A classic de luxe blend with a malty sweetness and a trace of peatiness in its flavours.

*C*hivas Brothers is a subsidiary of the Canadian drinks firm Seagram, by whom it was bought in 1949. The origins of the Chivas Brothers company can be traced back to the establishment of a wine and spirit merchant and licensed grocer in Aberdeen in 1801. Owning nine malt distilleries, Seagram is an important company in the Scotch whisky market. Chivas Regal is one of several Seagram blends which include Passport, 100 Pipers and the premium 21-year-old Royal Salute.

The Claymore

Whyte & Mackay, Glasgow

TYPE

Blend

STRENGTH

40%

TASTE RATING

2–3

MINIATURES

Yes

COMMENTS

A nicely rounded, medium-bodied blend with a mellow aroma and a well-balanced, smooth and rich taste.

VISITORS

The blending and bottling plant is not open to visitors.

*T*he Claymore is a popular blend which is owned by Whyte & Mackay, the blending and bottling company begun in 1882 by whisky merchants James Whyte and Charles Mackay. As with many of the company's whiskies, The Claymore is popular in export markets as well as in the UK, where it is among the best-selling blends. In 1993 Whyte & Mackay acquired Invergordon Distillers, adding seven malt distilleries (three of which have now been mothballed) and the big Invergordon grain distillery to their holdings.

Clynelish

Clynelish Distillery,
Brora, Sutherland

TYPE
Single malt

BOTTLING AGE
14 years

STRENGTH
43%

TASTE RATING
3

MINIATURES
Yes

COMMENTS
Clynelish is a medium-bodied, full-flavoured whisky with many devotees. It is slightly dry to the taste, with a hint of peat.

VISITORS
Visitors are welcome 0930–1630 Mon.–Fri. Telephone 01408-621444.

HIGHLAND
SINGLE MALT
SCOTCH WHISKY

One of the most northerly in Scotland.

CLYNELISH

distillery was established in Brora by the Marquess of STAFFORD in 1819. Its building signalled the end of illicit distilling in the area and provided a ready market for locally grown barley. Water is piped from the CLYNEMILTON burn to produce this fruity, & slightly smoky single MALT SCOTCH WHISKY much appreciated by connoisseurs

YEARS **14** OLD

43% vol   70cl

*T*his distillery had its origins in the early nineteenth century and was built by the man who became the first Duke of Sutherland, the prime mover in the most infamous of the Highland Clearances. Its purpose was to make full use of the cheap grain grown on the new coastal farms of his newly-cleared tenants. The distillery was bought by Ainslie and Heilbron in 1896. A new distillery was built on adjacent land in 1967–68, taking the name Clynelish, while the original distillery, now renamed Brora, was closed by the Distillers Company Ltd, its parent company, in 1983. It is now owned by United Distillers.

HIGHLAND
from
Coleburn-Glenlivet
Distillery
AGED 17 YEARS
Distilled March 1978 and Bottled October 1995
Matured in Oak Cask
PRODUCT OF SCOTLAND
HIGHLAND

70 cl   58% vol

Coleburn

Coleburn Distillery,
Longmorn, Elgin, Moray

TYPE

Single malt

BOTTLING AGE

Varies

STRENGTH

Varies

TASTE RATING

3

MINIATURES

Yes

COMMENTS

A difficult-to-find malt with a delicate, fragrant aroma and pleasant, slightly flowery taste. Available bottled by independent merchants.

*C*oleburn was built by John Robertson of Dundee in 1896 and was licensed to J. & G. Stewart, a subsidiary of the Distillers Company Ltd and blenders of Usher's whiskies. It was acquired by United Distillers and mothballed in 1985. Almost all of its produce went into blends, and since its closure, its malt has become even rarer.

Columba Cream

John Murray & Co (Mull),
Calgary, Isle of Mull

TYPE

Liqueur

BOTTLING AGE

4 years

STRENGTH

17%

TASTE RATING

2

MINIATURES

Yes

COMMENTS

A blend of five single malt whiskies, with the addition of honey and cream makes for a very pleasant and mellow whisky cream liqueur.

VISITORS

The plant is not open to visitors.

*J*ohn Murray & Co. have been producing Columba Cream for several years to a formula which is based on a traditional recipe. With five single malts included in its recipe, this high-quality cream liqueur is an exceptionally fine example of its type. The company has offices on the Isle of Mull, and blending and bottling is currently carried out at their plant in Perth.

Convalmore

Convalmore Distillery,
Dufftown, Keith, Banffshire

CONNOISSEURS CHOICE

Connoisseurs Choice, a range of single malts from various districts of Scotland.

The distilleries situated in the area of the valley of the River Spey produce some of the finest malt whiskies.

SINGLE SPEYSIDE MALT SCOTCH WHISKY
DISTILLED AT
CONVALMORE
DISTILLERY
Proprietors: W.P. Lowrie & Co. Ltd

DISTILLED **1969** DISTILLED

SPECIALLY SELECTED, PRODUCED AND BOTTLED BY
GORDON & MACPHAIL
ELGIN · SCOTLAND
PRODUCT OF SCOTLAND

70cl   40%vol

TYPE

Single malt

BOTTLING AGE

Varies

STRENGTH

Varies

TASTE RATING

3

MINIATURES

Yes

COMMENTS

𝒲 P. Lowrie, the present licensed distillers, bought Convalmore in 1904, eleven years after its founding. Considerably damaged by fire in 1909, it was rebuilt the following year when experiments were made in the production of malt whisky from patent stills; this was abandoned in 1916, however, in favour of the traditional pot-still method which was considered to mature the whisky better. Almost all the production of Convalmore goes into blends. The distillery was acquired by United Distillers and was mothballed in 1985.

Available only from independent merchants, this is a dry, aromatic, atypical Speyside malt which works best as a digestif.

Cragganmore

*Cragganmore Distillery,
Ballindalloch, Banffshire*

TYPE
Single malt

BOTTLING AGE
12 years

STRENGTH
40%

TASTE RATING
3–4

MINIATURES
Yes

COMMENTS
A Speyside malt of distinctive and complex character, Cragganmore has a delicate aroma and smoky finish.

VISITORS
The distillery is not open to visitors.

*C*ragganmore was built in 1869 and was the first distillery to be constructed alongside an existing railway and so utilise the then new mode of transport for distribution. The distillery took its name from nearby Craggan More Hill. It was built by John Smith (a man of great bulk, also known locally as 'Cragganmore') and is now licensed to D. & J. McCallum. Most of its production goes into blends, especially Old Parr, and until a few years ago, the single malt was only infrequently available. The distillery is owned by United Distillers.

Craigellachie

Craigellachie Distillery, Craigellachie, Aberlour, Banffshire

TYPE
Single malt

BOTTLING AGE
14 years

STRENGTH
43%

TASTE RATING
3

MINIATURES
Yes

COMMENTS

A smoky-smelling and -tasting malt of medium body, Craigellachie works well as an after-dinner dram. It is generally available from independent whisky merchants.

VISITORS

The distillery is not open to visitors.

*T*his distillery is pleasantly situated on high ground above the River Spey outside Dufftown. It was built in 1891 by the Craigellachie Distillery Co., a founder of which was Peter Mackie, the creator of the White Horse brand. Mackie and Co. (later White Horse Distillers) subsequently bought the distillery in 1915. It is now owned by United Distillers and most of its production is devoted to blending. The single malt is still relatively rare, only becoming available in official bottlings in the Distillery (Flora and Fauna) Malts series early in the 1990s.

Crawford's
Three Star

Whyte & Mackay
Glasgow

TYPE

Blend

STRENGTH

40%

TASTE RATING

2

MINIATURES

Yes

COMMENTS

A smooth, nicely balanced blend with light, malty flavours. The de luxe Five Star is a richer whisky with mild sherried hints.

A & A. Crawford was established as a whisky merchant and blenders in Leith in 1860. Although the original founders died before the end of the century, the business was taken over by their sons who were responsible for the launching of the successful Crawford's Three Star blend at the start of the century. The de luxe Five Star appeared in the 1920s and was also well received. The company was acquired by the Distillers Company Ltd in 1944 and ownership subsequently passed to Whyte & Mackay in 1986.

Cutty Sark

Berry Brothers & Rudd Ltd,
London

TYPE

Blend

STRENGTH

40%

TASTE RATING

2

MINIATURES

Yes

COMMENTS

*B*erry Brothers & Rudd, have been successful London wine and spirit merchants since the seventeenth century. Their Cutty Sark blend was launched in 1923 specifically for the American market, where it quickly became a brand leader, a position it has sustained ever since. It is also a leading premium blend in countries such as Greece, Japan, Portugal, Korea and Brazil. The whisky takes its name from the famous clipper ship built in Scotland in 1869, renowned as one of the fastest sailing ships of its day. The distinctive yellow label was designed by the Scottish artist, James McBey.

A delicate, smooth whisky with a fresh, crisp taste. A high proportion of oak-matured Speyside malts contributes greatly to its smooth taste.

Cutty Sark Emerald

*Berry Brothers & Rudd Ltd,
London*

TYPE
Blend

STRENGTH
43%

TASTE RATING
2

MINIATURES
Yes

COMMENTS
Cutty Sark Emerald has a soft,
honeyed fruit aroma, a hint of
sweetness on the palate and a
rounded, lengthy finish.

*B*erry Brothers & Rudd have
been successful London wine
and spirit merchants since the seventeenth century. The original Cutty
Sark blend was launched in 1923
specifically for the American market,
where it quickly became a brand
leader, a position it has sustained ever
since. A blend of oak-matured
whiskies of at least 12 years of age,
Cutty Sark Emerald has strong international following, particularly in
Japan, Korea, Portugal, Spain and
Greece.

Cutty Sark
Imperial Kindom Golden Jubilee

Berry Brothers & Rudd Ltd, London

TYPE
Blend

STRENGTH
43%

TASTE RATING
2–3

MINIATURES
No

COMMENTS
Exceptionally smooth, Golden Jubilee is a rich, fruity nosed whisky with a slightly sweet taste and a lingering finish.

*B*erry Brothers & Rudd have been successful London wine and spirit merchants since the seventeenth century. The original Cutty Sark blend was launched in 1923 specifically for the American market, where it quickly became a brand leader, a position it has sustained ever since. Imperial Kingdom Golden Jubilee is produced from Berry Bros & Rudd's own private whisky reserves and contains a some very fine rare whiskies over 50-years-old. Golden Jubilee is a commemoration of Queen Victoria's reign and the handsome gift-box packaging illustrates the achievements of that age.

Dailuaine

Dailuaine Distillery, Carron, Banffshire

TYPE
Single malt

BOTTLING AGE
16 years

STRENGTH
43%

TASTE RATING
4

MINIATURES
Yes

COMMENTS
This is a rare malt, with a heathery and sweetish flavour.

VISITORS
The distillery is not open to visitors.

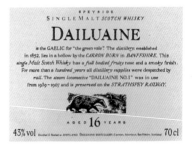

SPEYSIDE
SINGLE MALT *SCOTCH WHISKY*

DAILUAINE

is the GAELIC for "the green vale". The *distillery* established in 1852, lies in a hollow by the *CARRON BURN* in *BANFFSHIRE*. This *single Malt Scotch Whisky* has a *full bodied fruity* nose and a *smoky* finish. For more than a *hundred years* all *distillery supplies* were despatched by *rail*. The *steam locomotive* "DAILUAINE NO.1" was in use from 1939–1967 and is *preserved* on the *STRATHSPEY RAILWAY*.

AGED **16** YEARS

43% vol   70 cl

*D*ailuaine Distillery stands near the Spey below Ben Rinnes and was established in 1851 by William Mackenzie; it was subsequently taken over by his son, Thomas, and greatly expanded during the 1880s. The distillery was one several owned by the Dailuaine–Talisker Distillery Co., an amalgamated company formed by Mackenzie. Its current owners are United Distillers and most of its produce goes into their blends, such as Johnnie Walker. Consequently its single malt is still relatively rare, and has only become available in official bottlings in the Distillery (Flora and Fauna) Malts series early in the 1990s.

The Dalmore

Dalmore Distillery,
Alness, Ross-shire

TYPE

Single malt

BOTTLING AGE

12 years

STRENGTH

40%

TASTE RATING

4

MINIATURES

Yes

COMMENTS

A smooth, full-bodied whisky with a hint of sherry and peat in its malted flavours. A good digestif.

VISITORS

Visitors are welcome by appointment at 1100 or 1400 Mon., Tue., Thur., early Sept.– mid June. Telephone 01349-882362 to arrange.

*B*uilt in 1839, Dalmore Distillery was bought in 1867 by the Mackenzie family, although ownership has now passed to Whyte & Mackay. Much of its produce today goes into Whyte & Mackay blends. The distillery is attractively set in a picturesque location with a wooded, hilly backdrop and outlook over the Cromarty Firth to the fertile Black Isle, a location which meant a break in the production of whisky during the First World War when the American navy took over the distillery and its access to the deepwater Cromarty Firth, for the manufacture of mines.

Dalwhinnie

Dalwhinnie Distillery,
Dalwhinnie, Inverness-shire

TYPE
Single malt

BOTTLING AGE
15 years

STRENGTH
43%

TASTE RATING
2–3

MINIATURES
Yes

COMMENTS
Ideal as a pre- or post-dinner dram, Dalwhinnie is light and aromatic with a soft, heather-honey finish.

VISITORS
Visitors are welcome 0930–1700 Mon.–Fri. Telephone 01528-522264.

*B*uilt in 1898 at the end of the boom years for the whisky industry, what is today Dalwhinnie Distillery was called Strathspey when it first opened, even though it was not, strictly speaking, on Speyside. It stands on the Drumochter Pass at a height of more than 1000 feet, close to pure water sources, and was for many years Scotland's highest distillery. It is presently owned by United Distillers. Most of its output went to blending until 1988 when the Dalwhinnie single malt was developed.

Deanston

Deanston Distillery,
Doune, Stirlingshire

TYPE

Single malt

BOTTLING AGE

12, 17 years

STRENGTH

40%

TASTE RATING

3

MINIATURES

Yes

COMMENTS

A light, fresh, smooth Highland malt with a sweetish, fruity flavour.

VISITORS

The distillery is not open to visitors.

Originally a cotton mill dating from 1785, Deanston was converted to a whisky distillery in 1966. Water for distilling and electricity comes from the River Teith that rises north of Loch Lomond and flows through the Trossachs. The mill's original weaving sheds, with their humidity control and their temperature, are perfect for maturing the whisky and are considered to add a natural smoothness to its character. Deanston was bought by Burn Stewart of Glasgow in 1991.

Dewar's White Label

United Distillers,
Banbeath, Leven, Fife

TYPE

Blend

STRENGTH

40%

TASTE RATING

2

MINIATURES

Yes

COMMENTS

Dewar's White Label, the best-selling Scotch whisky in the USA, has a slightly smoky aroma and a complex, delicate, malty flavour with a clean, dry finish.

*J*ohn Dewar and Sons was one of the blending companies instrumental in the development of new whisky markets outside Scotland. Begun in Perth in 1846, it was the first company to sell its whisky in bottles as well as casks, thus opening up a new market in the home rather than just the licensed shop, pub or hotel. Dewar was also a pioneer of whisky advertising and was one of the first companies whose bottles carried its company name. By the time it became part of the Distillers Company Ltd in 1925, it owned seven distilleries, two of which (Aberfeldy and Glen Ord) are still licensed to Dewar. More than 90% of production is exported.

Dimple

United Distillers,
Banbeath, Leven, Fife

TYPE

De luxe

BOTTLING AGE

15 years

STRENGTH

40%

TASTE RATING

2–3

MINIATURES

Yes

COMMENTS

In its distinctive triangular bottle, Dimple is a good-quality de luxe blend which is also a leader in its market in the UK. More sophisticated than the standard Haig blend, it has a mellow sweetness which is harmoniously balanced by a smoky, peaty flavour.

*H*aig is a family name long associated with the whisky industry, going back almost 350 years, when Robert Haig, a farmer of Stirlingshire, was rebuked by his local kirk session for distilling his whisky on a Sunday. The Haigs were instrumental in introducing new practices and machinery (for example the new patent still in the 1830s) to the grain distilleries which they built in Edinburgh and elsewhere in the east. The company was acquired by the Distillers Company in 1919 and by United Distillers in 1986. Today Haig holds the licence for three malt distilleries: Glenkinchie, Glenlossie and Mannochmore, as well as Cameronbridge grain distillery in Fife.

Drambuie

Drambuie,
Kirkliston, West Lothian

TYPE

Liqueur

STRENGTH

40%

TASTE RATING

2

MINIATURES

Yes

COMMENTS

Based on a blend of secret ingredients, Drambuie is a sweet after-dinner whisky liqueur with a rich and creamy honeyed flavour complemented by fragrant, fruity notes.

VISITORS

The plant is not open to visitors.

rambuie is produced in the Lothians, having moved from its original home on Skye at the start of this century after the decision was taken to produce the liqueur commercially. Drambuie ('the drink that satisfies') is chronicled – perhaps with a keener eye on marketing than history – as being the personal liqueur of Prince Charles Edward Stuart, Bonnie Prince Charlie. After his army's defeat by the Hanoverian army at Culloden in 1746, the prince fled to Skye with a few supporters. Among them was Captain John Mackinnon, a native of Skye, whom the prince is said to have rewarded for his loyalty by giving him his only remaining possession – the secret recipe for his personal liqueur.

HIGHLAND
SINGLE MALT SCOTCH WHISKY

DUFFTOWN

distillery was established near *Dufftown* at the end of the C19th. The *bright flash* of the KINGFISHER can often be seen over the *DULLAN RIVER*, which flows past the old stone buildings of the distillery on its way *north* to the *SPEY*. This *single HIGHLAND MALT WHISKY* is typically *SPEYSIDE* in character with a *delicate, fragrant, almost flowery* aroma and taste which *lingers* on the palate.

43% vol   AGED **15** YEARS   70cl
Distilled & Bottled in *SCOTLAND* DUFFTOWN DISTILLERY, Dufftown, Keith, Banffshire, Scotland

Dufftown

Dufftown Distillery, Dufftown, Keith, Banffshire

TYPE
Single malt

BOTTLING AGE
15 years

STRENGTH
43%

TASTE RATING
2–3

MINIATURES
Yes

COMMENTS
A pleasant Speyside malt with a delicate, fragrant aroma which is almost flowery, and a smooth, sweet taste. Doubles as a before- or after-dinner dram.

VISITORS
Visitors are welcome by appointment, 0900–1600. Larger parties should telephone in advance. Telephone 01340-820224 to arrange.

*P*rettily situated at the water's edge in the Dullan Glen, this is one of seven distilleries in and around Dufftown, a major whisky production centre with plentiful resources of water, peat and, previously, barley. Despite the abundance of fresh water in the glen, there were disputes in the early years over water rights, some of which led to the nocturnal diversion and re-diversion of local supplies. The distillery finally gained the right to draw its supplies from Jock's Well, a reliable source of fine, sweet water some distance away. The single malt is still relatively rare, becoming more widely available in official bottlings in United Distillers' Distillery (Flora and Fauna) Malts series early in the 1990s.

Dunhill
Old Master

Justerini & Brooks,
London

TYPE

Blend

STRENGTH

43%

TASTE RATING

3

MINIATURES

Yes

COMMENTS

A combination of some thirty individual whiskies, some more than twenty years old, Dunhill Old Master is an exceptionally smooth, richly flavoured blend.

*J*usterini & Brooks' was established in London by the Italian wine merchant, Giacomo Justerini, in 1749 and began selling Scotch whisky thirty years later. In 1962 the company built on previous amalgamations by combining with W. & A. Gilbey to form International Distillers and Vintners Ltd (IDV). Grand Metropolitan bought IDV, then part of Watney Mann & Truman, in 1972. J&B have created a range of high-quality premium whiskies for Alfred Dunhill Ltd, including Dunhill Centenary, Dunhill's Celebration Edition and Dunhill's Gentlemen's Speyside Blend.

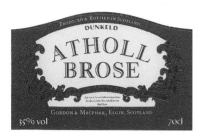

Dunkeld
Atholl Brose

Gordon and MacPhail,
Elgin, Moray

TYPE

Liqueur

BOTTLING AGE

12 years

STRENGTH

35%

TASTE RATING

2

MINIATURES

Yes

COMMENTS

G ordon and MacPhail started in business in 1895 as a licensed grocers and wine and spirit merchant. Unlike many other similar contemporary companies, they have retained all the original aspects of their business as well as extending into vatting, blending and bottling, and are unique in maturing all their whiskies from new. They recently moved into distillation with the purchase of Benromach Distillery from United Distillers. They also produce this liqueur, which won a Silver Award (1985) at the International Wine and Spirit Competition and a Gold Award (1987), when it was named 'the best liqueur in the world'.

Based on a traditional recipe, this liqueur has a good whisky association coming through its sweetness. It is herbal on the nose, with a long, warming finish.

VISITORS

Gordon and MacPhail's shop, South St, Elgin is open 0900–1715 Mon.–Wed. (0900–1300 Wed. in winter), 0830–1715 Thu.–Fri., 0900–1700 Sat.

The Edradour

Edradour Distillery,
Pitlochry, Perthshire

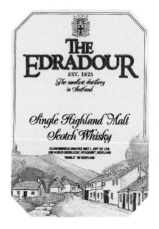

TYPE

Single malt

BOTTLING AGE

10 years

STRENGTH

40%

TASTE RATING

3

MINIATURES

Yes

COMMENTS

The Edradour is a smooth Highland malt with pleasant notes of fruit and malt in its taste, complemented by a slight dryness.

VISITORS

Visitors are welcome. Telephone 01796-472095 to arrange.

*E*dradour is Scotland's smallest distillery, as well as being one of its most picturesque. Built in 1837, it stands on the steep banks of a burn in the Perthshire countryside, and sympathetic modernization in 1982 left its appearance unchanged. The distillery had been bought by William Whiteley in 1933 and, despite a takeover in 1982 by Pernod Ricard subsidiary the House of Campbell, Whiteley still hold the licence. Most of the malt goes into their blends House of Lords and Clan Campbell, and it is only since 1986 that The Edradour has been available as a single malt under the distillery label.

Fairlie's

Glenturret Distillery,
The Hosh, Perthshire

TYPE
Liqueur

BOTTLING AGE
24%

TASTE RATING
2

MINIATURES
No

COMMENTS
Smooth and delicate without being cloying, the secret recipe used to produce this unique drink allows the top-grade malt used to come through. Excellent as a mixer.

VISITORS
Visitors are welcome all year. Telephone 01764-656565

*F*airlie's Light Highland Liqueur is produced at Glenturret Distillery, situated in one of Perthshire's most spectacular Highland settings. It is named after the family which did so much to resurrect the distillery's fortunes in the 1960s. The label sports a pouncing cat motif and paw prints in honour of Towser, the late distillery cat whose record of 28,899 mice caught in a career lasting almost twenty-four years earned her a place in the *Guinness Book of Records* as the world's most successful mouser.

The Famous Grouse

Matthew Gloag and Son,
Perth, Perthshire

TYPE
Blend

STRENGTH
40%

TASTE RATING
2

MINIATURES
Yes

COMMENTS

The Famous Grouse is a light-to-medium-bodied whisky with a fresh smoothness and a pleasant, lightly peated flavour. It has been the most popular blend in Scotland for several years.

$\mathcal{M}$atthew Gloag & Son began trading in Perth in 1800 as a licensed grocers, acquiring interests in blending and bottling as the firm expanded during the nineteenth century. What became their most famous product appeared at the end of the century, with the grouse on the name and label successfully capitalizing on the popularity of sporting pastimes among Victorian and Edwardian gentlemen. The blend celebrated its first century in 1995. The company was bought by Highland Distilleries in 1970 and received the benefits of wider distribution and advertising. Highland Distilleries own Bunnahabhain, Glenglassaugh, Glen Rothes, Highland Park and Tamdhu malt distilleries.

FRASER McDONALD'S

70 cl℮   40% vol

Rare   Old

BLENDED

SCOTCH WHISKY

DISTILLED BLENDED & BOTTLED
IN SCOTLAND BY
FRASER MacDONALD DISTILLERY CO LTD

LONDON · GLASGOW

Fraser McDonald

*Gibson Scotch Whisky Ltd,
Glasgow*

TYPE
Blend

STRENGTH
40%

TASTE RATING
2–3

MINIATURES
No

COMMENTS
Fraser McDonald is a smooth and mellow blend whose light, fresh taste is underlain by gentle peaty notes.

*F*raser McDonald is, along with Scotia Royale and Royal Culross, one of the blends of Gibson Scotch Whisky Co. Ltd, who operate as a subsidiary of the Loch Lomond Distillery Co. Ltd, producers of Inchmurrin single malt. As well as a new grain complex at Loch Lomond, the company holds three malt distilleries: the two Lowland distilleries of Loch Lomond at Alexandria and Littlemill at Bowling, and Glen Scotia in Campbeltown. The latter two have now been mothballed.

Glayva

*Glayva Liqueur,
Leith, Edinburgh*

TYPE
Liqueur

STRENGTH
35%

BOTTLING AGE
2

MINIATURES
Yes

COMMENTS
Glayva, whose name derives from the Gaelic for 'very good', is a rich, syrupy-textured after-dinner liqueur with a hint of tangerine in its sweet flavours.

VISITORS
The plant is not open to visitors.

Glayva was originally created by Ronald Morrison & Co., an Edinburgh merchants well versed in flavours and bouquets. The liqueur's distinctive combination of aged whisky, syrup of herbs, aromatic oils and honey took many years to perfect. The ownership of Glayva passed to Whyte & Mackay in 1993 when they acquired Invergordon Distillers, who themselves had owned the brand since 1984. This is one of the biggest sellers in the Scotch whisky liqueur market.

Glen Albyn

Glen Albyn Distillery,
Inverness, Inverness-shire

TYPE
Single malt

STRENGTH
Varies

BOTTLING AGE
Varies

TASTE RATING
3

MINIATURES
Yes

COMMENTS
This whisky is available from independent bottlers only and is difficult to come by. It is a medium-bodied, smooth malt with a hint of smokiness in its bouquet and taste.

*G*len Albyn was first established by a provost of Inverness in 1840, only to be turned into a flour mill after two decades of distilling. It was re-established in the 1880s when a new Glen Albyn Distillery was built in another site close to the Caledonian Canal. The distillery was bought by Mackinlay and Birnie (who also owned the neighbouring Glen Mhor Distillery) in 1920 and was transferred to Scottish Malt Distillers (SMD), a subsidiary of the Distillers Company Ltd, in 1972. Glen Albyn was one of several SMD distilleries closed down in 1983 and it was subsequently demolished by United Distillers in 1988.

Glenburgie

The Glenburgie-Glenlivet Distillery, Forres, Moray

TYPE
Single malt

STRENGTH
Varies

BOTTLING AGE
Varies

TASTE RATING
3

MINIATURES
Yes

COMMENTS
A light-bodied, delicate single malt whose sweet, slightly floral taste makes it ideal as an aperitif. It is found relatively rarely in this country, as most goes for export.

VISITORS
The distillery has no reception centre but visitors are welcome by appointment. Telephone 01343-850258 to arrange.

A distillery was said to have been established here in 1810, but production ceased and was not revived until the second half of the nineteenth century. It was bought by James & George Stodart Ltd of Dumbarton who themselves were taken over by Hiram Walker in the 1930s. The distillery was extended in 1958 and is now owned by Allied Distillers, with most of its produce going into their blends.

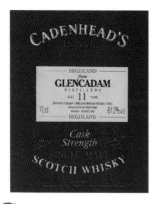

Glencadam

*Glencadam Distillery,
Brechin, Angus*

TYPE
Single malt

STRENGTH
Varies

BOTTLING AGE
Varies

TASTE RATING
3–4

MINIATURES
Yes

COMMENTS
Glencadam, generally available from independent whisky merchants, has a delicate, fruity bouquet and rich, sweetish flavour with a smooth, well-rounded finish.

VISITORS
The distillery has no reception centre but visitors are welcome by appointment. Telephone 01356-622217 to arrange.

*G*lencadam, built around 1825, dates from the time of the first wave of licensed distilleries, and was one of two distilleries in Brechin dating from this decade (North Port being the other). It takes its water from Moorfoot Loch. It is owned by Allied Distillers but has only rarely been officially bottled as a single malt, with most of its production going into the blend Stewart's Cream of the Barley.

Glen Calder

Gordon and MacPhail,
Elgin, Moray

TYPE
Blend

STRENGTH
40%

TASTE RATING
2

MINIATURES
Yes

COMMENTS
A very pleasant blend with a smooth, honey-like nose and light, slightly smoky finish.

VISITORS
Gordon and MacPhail's shop, South St, Elgin is open 0900–1715 Mon.–Wed. (0900–1300 Wed. in winter), 0830–1715 Thu.–Fri., 0900–1700 Sat. Telephone 01340-871471.

Gordon and MacPhail started in business in 1895 as a licensed grocers and wine and spirit merchant, as had done so many of the foremost names among the Scotch whisky blending industry. Unlike the others, however, Gordon and MacPhail have retained all the original aspects of their business as well as extending into vatting, blending and bottling, and they are today the world's leading malt whisky specialists. Some of the formulas for their blends date from the turn of the century. Glen Calder is one of the most popular blends in northern Scotland and won a Silver Award at the 1981 International Wine and Spirits Competition.

Glen Deveron

Macduff Distillery,
Banff, Banffshire

TYPE
Single malt

BOTTLING AGE
12 years

STRENGTH
40%

TASTE RATING
3–4

MINIATURES
Yes

COMMENTS
A very pleasant Highland malt with a smooth, mellow taste and fresh bouquet.

VISITORS
Visitors are welcome by appointment. Telephone 01261-812612 to arrange.

A modern distillery, built in 1960, Macduff is one of the few distilleries to give its single malt a different name from its own (although independent bottlers do market the whisky, including miniatures, under the name of 'Macduff'). The malt takes its names from the nearby River Deveron from which is drawn the water used for cooling in the production process. Macduff Distillery is now owned by William Lawson Distillers, a subsidiary of Bacardi Ltd, Bermuda.

Glendronach

The Glendronach Distillery,
Forgue, Huntly,
Aberdeenshire

TYPE
Single malt

BOTTLING AGE
12 years

STRENGTH
40%, 43%

TASTE RATING
3

MINIATURES
Yes

COMMENTS
Glendronach is a beautifully rounded single malt whose slight peaty tones are balanced by a lingering sweetness.

VISITORS
Visitors are welcome by appointment. Telephone 01466-730202 to arrange.

*T*his distillery, set picturesquely on the Dronach Burn in the Aberdeenshire countryside, is one of the most attractive in the Highlands. Built in 1826, it was one of the first to be licensed, and its whisky enjoyed a wide reputation in the nineteenth century. Its original hand-turned malting floor and coal-fired stills have been retained. Since 1960 it has been operated by William Teacher & Sons, with produce going into the Teacher's blends. It has been owned since 1988 by Allied Distillers who have temporarily suspended production.

Glendullan

*Glendullan Distillery,
Dufftown, Keith, Banffshire*

TYPE
Single malt

BOTTLING AGE
12 years

STRENGTH
43%

TASTE RATING
3

MINIATURES
Yes

COMMENTS
A good single malt with a robust character yet a mellow, fruity flavour.

VISITORS
Visitors are welcome by appointment. Telephone 01340-820250 to arrange.

*T*his is one of the seven Dufftown distilleries, built just before the turn of the century and picturesquely set on the banks of the Fiddich. Built for William Williams of Aberdeen, it passed to the control of Macdonald Greenlees & Williams after the First World War and, with its parent company, into the ownership of the Distillers Company Ltd in 1926. It is now owned by United Distillers and its single malt is still relatively rare, although it has been officially bottled in the Distillery (Flora and Fauna) Malts series. Glendullan is also an important component of Old Parr and of President, a de luxe blend.

Glenfarclas

*Glenfarclas Distillery,
Marypark, Ballindalloch,
Banffshire*

TYPE
Single malt

BOTTLING AGE
10, 12, 15, 21, 25, 30 years

STRENGTH
40%, 43%, 46%, 60%

TASTE RATING
3–4, 5 (60%)

MINIATURES
10 years old and
105 cask strength

COMMENTS
A whisky of true character, Glenfarclas is widely acknowledged as one of the classic malts. It has a rich, sherry bouquet, a well-rounded, fruity body and a delicious, mellow finish.

VISITORS
Visitors are welcome 0900–1630 Mon.–Fri., 1000–1600 Sat., June–Sept., 1000–1600 Mon.–Fri., Oct.– May; or by appointment. Large parties should telephone in advance. Telephone 01807-500209.

*G*lenfarclas is one of the few independently owned distilleries left in the Highlands. Founded in 1836, it was bought in 1865 by J. & G. Grant (who were no direct relations of the family of Grants at Glenfiddich) and is still in family hands. Glenfarclas bottles a wide range of malts of varying ages and strengths. The distillery is set in an isolated spot by Ben Rinnes yet it attracts in excess of 60,000 visitors a year to its well-maintained visitor facilities.

Glenfiddich

Glenfiddich Distillery,
Dufftown, Keith, Banffshire

TYPE
Single malt

BOTTLING AGE
No age given

STRENGTH
40%

TASTE RATING
2

MINIATURES
Yes

COMMENTS
Glenfiddich has a light, peaty aroma with a smooth, counter-balancing sweetness. It offers an excellent introduction to malt whisky, and is ideal, too, as an aperitif.

VISITORS
Visitors are welcome 0930–1630 Mon.–Fri. all year; 0930–1630 Sat., 1200–1630 Sun., Easter–mid Oct. Large parties should telephone in advance. Telephone 01340-820373.

*G*lenfiddich Distillery was started by William Grant, a former apprentice shoemaker who worked at Mortlach, another Dufftown distillery, until he gained enough knowledge and money to set up on his own in 1887. The new distillery was successful as soon as it went into production, and has remained so ever since, thanks not only to the quality and accessibility of its product but also to far-sighted marketing which has made its single malt possibly the best-known in the world. The distillery is part of the largest family-owned independent whisky company.

Glen Garioch

Glengarioch Distillery,
Oldmeldrum, Aberdeenshire

TYPE
Single malt

BOTTLING AGE
9, 15, 21 years

STRENGTH
40%, 43%

TASTE RATING
3

MINIATURES
Yes

COMMENTS
This medium-bodied whisky, with its light texture and smoky flavour, is an ideal after-dinner dram.

AGED FIFTEEN YEARS
GLEN GARIOCH
HIGHLAND
Single Malt
SCOTCH WHISKY
DISTILLED & BOTTLED IN SCOTLAND
70cl e   43%Vol

Set in the small Aberdeenshire market town of Oldmeldrum, Glengarioch was reputedly founded in the 1790s. It has had several owners throughout its history, and was sold by the Distillers Company Ltd in 1970 to Morrison, two years after its closure because of a shortage of water. Having sunk a new well, Morrison were able to tap sufficient sources of spring water to enable normal production to continue. The distillery has now been mothballed and its long-term future seems uncertain.

Glengoyne

*Glengoyne Distillery,
Dumgoyne, Stirlingshire*

TYPE
Single malt

BOTTLING AGE
10, 12, 17 years

STRENGTH
40%, 43%

TASTE RATING
2–3

MINIATURES
Yes

COMMENTS
A light, pleasant, sweetish whisky with a fragrant aroma and no abrasive edges. Ideal as an aperitif.

VISITORS
Visitors are welcome during working hours, Mon.–Sat. Large parties (of ten and over) are requested to book ahead. Telephone 01360-550254 to arrange.

*G*lengoyne stands just north of the Highland Line (the line initiated by the Customs and Excise to differentiate area boundaries between styles of whisky) and so qualifies as a Highland distillery. It was built in 1833 at the foot of the Campsie Fells, near the fifty-foot waterfall from which it takes its supplies. It was bought by Lang Brothers in 1876 and was sympathetically restored and extended in the 1960s.

Glen Grant

Glen Grant Distillery, Rothes, Moray

TYPE

Single malt

BOTTLING AGE

No age, 5, 10 years

STRENGTH

40%, 43%

TASTE RATING

2

MINIATURES

Yes

COMMENTS

The 5-year-old is light and dry, making it ideal as an aperitif, while the older version has a sweeter, fruitier, more rounded character.

VISITORS

Visitors are welcome 1000–1600 Mon.–Sat., and from 1230 Sun., mid Mar.–Oct. Telephone 01542-783318.

Opened by James and John Grant in 1840, Glen Grant enjoyed continuous expansion throughout the last century, and this has continued to the present day. The company was amalgamated with the Smiths of Glenlivet in the 1950s to form The Glenlivet and Glen Grant Distillers, which in turn merged with the Edinburgh blending firm of Hill Thomson in 1970 to form The Glenlivet Distillers. Glen Grant is now part of Seagram. The distillery's Five Years Old single malt is the best-selling malt whisky in Italy.

CONNOISSEURS CHOICE

Connoisseurs Choice, a range of single malts from various districts of Scotland

In the Highlands are situated the greatest number of malt whisky distilleries

SINGLE HIGHLAND MALT SCOTCH WHISKY
DISTILLED AT
GLEN KEITH
Distillery
Proprietors: The Chivas Bros. Ltd.

DISTILLED **1967** DISTILLED

70cl

SPECIALLY SELECTED, PRODUCED AND BOTTLED BY
GORDON & MACPHAIL
ELGIN · SCOTLAND
PRODUCT OF SCOTLAND

40% vol

Glen Keith

Glen Keith Distillery, Keith, Banffshire

TYPE

Single malt

BOTTLING AGE

Varies

STRENGTH

43%

TASTE RATING

2

MINIATURES

Yes

COMMENTS

A difficult-to-find, smooth and sweet-tasting Speyside single malt which is occasionally available from independent bottlers.

VISITORS

The distillery is open by appointment. Telephone 01542-783042 to arrange.

*G*len Keith was built by Chivas Brothers in 1958, across the River Isla from Strathisla, another of their distilleries and one of the oldest in Scotland. As if by deliberate contrast, processes used at Glen Keith are innovative, and it was the first of the Scotch whisky distilleries to have its production processes automated. Unlike the usual practice, distillations are not bottled at fixed ages but are individually selected at what is judged to be the optimum point in the maturation process.

Glenkinchie

*Glenkinchie Distillery,
Pencaitland, Tranet,
East Lothian*

TYPE

Single malt

BOTTLING AGE

10 years

STRENGTH

43%

TASTE RATING

3

MINIATURES

Yes

COMMENTS

Ideal as an aperitif, Glenkinchie, the Edinburgh malt, is the driest and smokiest of Lowland whiskies. It is a fine, pale, smooth whisky.

VISITORS

Visitors are welcome 0930–1630 Mon.–Fri. Telephone 01875-340333.

Glenkinchie takes its name from the burn which flows by it and the glen in which it stands. It was established in the late 1830s and has been in production since, except during the wars. The licence is held by Haig, the brand owned by United Distillers, and most of Glenkinchie's product goes into their blends. The single malt was officially bottled by United Distillers in their Classic Malts series.

The Glenlivet

The Glenlivet Distillery,
Ballindalloch, Banffshire

TYPE

Single malt

BOTTLING AGE

12, 18, 21 years

STRENGTH

40%, 43%

TASTE RATING

3–4

MINIATURES

Yes

COMMENTS

*T*his was one of the first distilleries licensed under the reforming 1823 Licensing Act – a fact which so incensed his still-illegal neighbours that its founder, George Smith, was obliged to carry pistols for his own protection. The whisky so grew in popularity that other distillers adopted the name, and an ensuing legal case and settlement (which endures to this day) allowed the Smiths to use the direct article in their whisky's name while others were to use it as a hyphenated suffix.

The Glenlivet is a subtly balanced malt. Its light, delicate bouquet has traces of fruit, and floral notes, while the complex flavours are delicately balanced between a medium sweetness and smooth dryness.

VISITORS

Visitors are welcome 1000–1600 Mon.–Sat., mid Mar.–end Oct., 1000–1800 Mon.–Sat. and from 1230 Sun., July–Aug. Telephone 01542-783220.

Glenlochy

Glenochy Distillery,
Fort William, Inverness-shire

CONNOISSEURS CHOICE

Connoisseurs Choice, a range of single malts from various districts of Scotland.

In the Highlands are situated the greatest number of malt whisky distilleries.

SINGLE HIGHLAND
MALT SCOTCH WHISKY
DISTILLED AT
GLENLOCHY
DISTILLERY
PROPRIETORS: D. & J. McCallum Ltd

DISTILLED 1977 DISTILLED

SPECIALLY SELECTED, PRODUCED AND BOTTLED BY
GORDON & MACPHAIL
ELGIN · SCOTLAND
PRODUCT OF SCOTLAND

70cl   40%vol

TYPE
Single malt

BOTTLING AGE
Varies

STRENGTH
Varies

TASTE RATING
2

MINIATURES
Yes

COMMENTS

A floral bouquet leads into a clean, dryish-tasting malt with a rather quick finish. Light-bodied and good as an aperitif.

Glenlochy Distillery was built close to Loch Lochy at the southern end of the Caledonian Canal in a pretty setting on the outskirts of Fort William. It was built in 1900 with production beginning the following year. The single malt is now something of a rarity, as almost all of the distillery's produce went into blends. The situation will not improve, as Glenlochy was closed by its parent company, United Distillers, in the 1980s, and sold outside the industry in 1991.

Glenlossie

Glenlossie-Glenlivet Distillery, Birnie, Elgin, Moray

TYPE

Single malt

BOTTLING AGE

10 years

STRENGTH

43%

TASTE RATING

2

MINIATURES

Yes

COMMENTS

Another whisky which is difficult to find, Glenlossie has a fresh, grassy aroma with a touch of fruitiness and a smooth, lingering flavour.

VISITORS

Visitors are welcome by appointment. Telephone 01343-86331 to arrange.

*G*lenlossie was built not far from the River Lossie in 1876 by a former distillery manager-turned-hotel owner from Lhanbryde, near Elgin. It was expanded and improved between 1896 and 1917. In 1962, its stills were increased from four to six, while in 1992 a new mash tun was fitted. The licensee is presently Haig and the distillery is owned by United Distillers. The single malt is still relatively rare, but became available in official bottlings in UD's Distillery (Flora and Fauna) Malts series early in the 1990s.

Glen Mhor

*Glen Mhor Distillery,
Inverness, Inverness-shire*

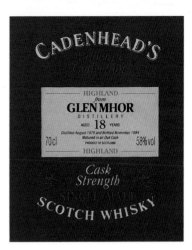

TYPE

Single malt

BOTTLING AGE

Varies

STRENGTH

Varies

TASTE RATING

3

MINIATURES

Yes

COMMENTS

Smooth and medium-bodied, Glen Mhor has a pleasant, subtle sweetness complemented by a dryish, heathery aftertaste.

*T*his distillery was built between 1892 and 1894 by Mackinlay and Birnie who were later to own the neighbouring Glen Albyn Distillery; John Birnie had previously managed Glen Albyn. Glen Mhor used the same water (from Loch Ness) and peat as its neighbour, but their whiskies were quite different. It was one of the first distilleries in Scotland to introduce mechanical malting in the late 1940s. It was also one of the Scottish Malt Distillers distilleries closed down by the Distillers Company Ltd in 1983, and was demolished in 1988.

Glenmorangie

Glenmorangie Distillery,
Tain, Ross-shire

TYPE
Single malt

BOTTLING AGE
10, 18 years

STRENGTH
40%, 43%

TASTE RATING
3–4

MINIATURES
Yes

COMMENTS

A smooth and medium bodied whisky, with a delicate, slightly sweet aroma. Scotland's best-selling single malt.

VISITORS

Visitors are welcome 1000–1600 Mon.–Fri., Apr.–Oct., 1400–1600 Mon–Fri., Nov.–Mar., or by appointment. Telephone 01862-892477 to arrange.

*D*istilling was begun here in 1843 by the Mathieson family as a sideline to farming. In 1918, The Glenmorangie Distillery Company passed into the control of its present owners, Macdonald and Muir Ltd. Water is supplied by unusually hard, mineral-rich springs in nearby Tarlogie Forest, and the lightly peated new spirit is distilled in Glenmorangie's characteristically tall, swan-necked stills, before being transferred into charred American oak barrels for the maturation process.

Glenmorangie
Port Wood Finish

*Glenmorangie Distillery,
Tain, Ross-shire*

TYPE
Single Malt

BOTTLING AGE
At least 12 years

STRENGTH
43%

TASTE RATING
3

MINIATURES
Yes

COMMENTS
This whisky has a sweet aroma with minty notes and a dry, very smooth taste. The port flavours of the final maturing process come through on the lingering and quite satisfying finish.

VISITORS
Visitors are welcome 1000–1600 Mon.–Fri., Apr.–Oct., 1400–1600 Mon–Fri., Nov.–Mar., or by appointment. Telephone 01862-892477 to arrange.

*T*his malt is one of a series of newcomers to Glenmorangie's single malts range. In its final 'finishing'period of maturation, the whisky is transferred not into the usual char-rec American oak bourbon barrels, but into casks which have previously contained port. This second wood imparts its own new qualities which enhance, without overpowering, the delicate and subtle core flavours. Glenmorangie also produce two other single malts which have been aged in Madeira and sherry casks.

Glen Moray

*Glen Moray-Glenlivet
Distillery,
Elgin, Moray*

TYPE
Single malt

BOTTLING AGE
12, 15 years

STRENGTH
40%, 43%

TASTE RATING
2–3

MINIATURES
Yes

COMMENTS

Golden in colour, with a soft, fresh bouquet leading into a smooth and rounded taste, Glen Moray is a classic Speyside malt. Ideal for drinking at any time, it is the sister malt to the better-known Glenmorangie.

VISITORS

Visitors are welcome by appointment. Telephone 01343-542577 to arrange.

*E*stablished during the whisky boom years of the 1890s, the Glen Moray-Glenlivet Distillery was expanded in 1958. Since the 1920s it has been owned by Macdonald & Muir Ltd and, in addition to its availability as a single malt, its produce also features in many well-known blends. Glen Moray is the sister distillery to the better-known Glenmorangie.

Glen Ord

Glen Ord Distillery,
Muir of Ord, Ross-shire

TYPE
Single malt

BOTTLING AGE
12 years

STRENGTH
40%

TASTE RATING
2–3

MINIATURES
Yes

COMMENTS
A smooth, well-rounded and slightly dry malt with a fragrant bouquet and mellow finish.

VISITORS
Visitors are welcome 0930–1700 Mon.–Fri. Telephone 01463-870421.

*T*his distillery stands in an area which was infamous for illicit distillation even as late as a century ago. It stands on a tributary of the River Conan, the Oran Burn, whose clear waters have been used by legal and illegal whisky producers alike. Ord Distillery, as it then was, was founded in 1838 on land leased from the Mackenzies of Ord to provide a ready market for barley produced on Mackenzie farms. It was acquired by Dewar in 1923, and is now owned by United Distillers.

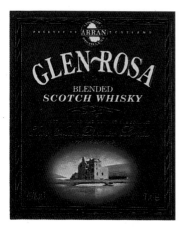

Glen Rosa

*Isle of Arran Distillers,
Mauchline, Ayrshire*

TYPE

Blend

STRENGTH

40%

TASTE RATING

2–3

MINIATURES

Yes

COMMENTS

*I*sle of Arran Distillers are a dynamic new player in the Scotch whisky industry. Independent and family-run, the company has a portfolio of blended and malt whiskies which has been successfully marketed throughout Europe, the Americas and Asia. In 1995 the company opened a new distillery on Arran at Lochranza and its first produce is presently maturing, with an expected launch as a single malt early in the new millenium.

Named after one of the most spectacular glens on Arran, this is a smooth and mellow medium-bodied blend.

The Glenrothes

*Glen Rothes Distillery,
Rothes, Moray*

TYPE
Single malt

BOTTLING AGE
Varies

STRENGTH
43%

TASTE RATING
3–4

MINIATURES
Yes

COMMENTS
A popular, full-bodied single malt with a delicate, lightly peated aroma and a pleasingly smooth aftertaste.

VISITORS
The distillery is not open to visitors.

*T*he Glen Rothes Distillery was built in 1878 for William Grant & Sons with the backing of a group of local businessmen, including the provost of Rothes. It was bought in 1887 by the Islay Distillery Company, owners of Bunnahabhain, and then became part of the Highland Distilleries company. They still own the distillery today. Glen Rothes has been expanded twice in the last thirty years. The Glen Rothes single malt is produced and distributed by Berry Brothers & Rudd, the owners of Cutty Sark whisky, in which Glen Rothes also features.

Glen Scotia

*Glen Scotia Distillery,
Campbeltown, Argyllshire*

TYPE

Single malt

BOTTLING AGE

12 years

STRENGTH

40%

TASTE RATING

3

MINIATURES

Yes

COMMENTS

Glen Scotia is a rich, peaty, oily malt with a pungent aroma and a smooth, well-rounded finish.

VISITORS

The distillery is not open to visitors.

Scotia, as it was previously known, was one of thirty-two Campbeltown distilleries operating last century, partly explaining why the town has its own regional classification, even though only two distilleries remain. Glen Scotia Distillery was built in 1835 and has had many owners, the ghost of one of whom is said to haunt the place. It is currently owned by Loch Lomond Distillery Co. Ltd, the owners of Loch Lomond Distillery and the producers of Inchmurrin single malt. Both Glen Scotia and its sister distillery, Littlemill at Bowling, have now been mothballed.

Glentauchers

*Glentauchers Distillery,
Mulben, Banffshire*

TYPE
Single malt

BOTTLING AGE
Varies

STRENGTH
40%

TASTE RATING
2

MINIATURES
Yes

COMMENTS

The sweetness of Glentauchers'
aroma and taste are balanced
by the light dryness of its finish. A nice pre-dinner dram,
but generally available only
from independent merchants.

VISITORS

The distillery has no reception
centre but visitors are welcome
by appointment. Telephone
01542-860272 to arrange.

*G*lentauchers was built in 1898 by
James Buchanan, the entrepreneur responsible for the success of
Black & White whisky, and its product
went into their blends. Buchanan was
a larger-than-life figure: in 1920 the
then PM Lloyd George offered him
the title, Lord Woolavington, in return
for a healthy donation to Liberal Party
funds. Buchanan was keen to take up
his offer but, in keeping with his own
business acumen and Lloyd George's
reputation, he signed his cheque
'Woolavington'. Buchanan's distillery
was largely rebuilt and modernized in
1965 but was silent for several years in
the 1980s until Allied Distillers
acquired it from United Distillers in
1988 and immediately reopened it.

The Glenturret

*Glenturret Distillery,
The Hosh, Creiff, Perthshire*

TYPE

Single malt

BOTTLING AGE

12, 15, 21, 25 years

STRENGTH

40%

TASTE RATING

3–4

MINIATURES

Yes

COMMENTS

Glenturret is an award-winning, full-bodied Highland malt with a rich, nutty flavour and nicely rounded finish.

VISITORS

Visitors are welcome all year. Telephone 01764-656565.

Glenturret stands in a lovely position on the banks of the River Turret, in an area where smuggling and illicit distillation were rife in the past. It is probable that the distillery's own eighteenth-century origins lie there; some of its buildings date from that time. Glenturret was closed and partially dismantled in the 1920s until 1959, when it was largely rebuilt, anticipating the huge upswing in demand for blended whiskies in the 1960s. Today its visitor facilities are among the best of any Scots whisky distillery.

The Glenturret
Original Malt Liqueur

Glenturret Distillery,
The Hosh, Creiff, Perthshire

TYPE

Liqueur

STRENGTH

35%

TASTE RATING

3

MINIATURES

Yes

COMMENTS

A blend of herbs and The Glenturret single malt produce a smooth, delicately flavoured drink that can be enjoyed on its own or as a base for mixers.

VISITORS

Visitors are welcome all year. Telephone 01764-656565.

*T*he Glenturret Original Malt Liqueur is produced at Scotland's oldest working distillery, officially established in 1775 but with a history predating this by some sixty years. Glenturret Distillery stands in a lovely position on the banks of the River Turret, in an area where smuggling and illicit distillation were rife in the past. Glenturret was closed from the 1920s until 1959, when it was largely rebuilt and its fortunes restored under the direction of the Fairlie family. Facilities for visitors are among the best of any distillery.

Glenugie

Glenugie Distillery,
Peterhead, Aberdeenshire

TYPE

Single malt

BOTTLING AGE

Varies

STRENGTH

Varies

TASTE RATING

2

MINIATURES

Yes

COMMENTS

A medium-bodied whisky with a sweetish, malty flavour and a fruity aroma. Available from independent bottlers.

*G*lenugie was the easternmost distillery in Scotland, located in the Peterhead, the fishing capital of the north-east. The distillery was first established in the 1830s, and was completely rebuilt in 1875. Although enjoyable, its produce never attained the status of a classic. Glenugie Distillery was closed permanently in 1982 and sold outside the industry. Although there were never any official bottlings under the its own label, supplies from the independent merchants are still available.

Grand Macnish

Macduff International,
Glasgow

TYPE
Blend

STRENGTH
40%, 43%

TASTE RATING
2

MINIATURES
Yes

COMMENTS
A light, very smooth blend in which the sweetness of the predominantly Highland whiskies comes through on the finish.

VISITORS
The blending and bottling plant is not open to visitors.

Grand MacNish is produced by Macduff International Ltd, an independent Scotch whisky company. The brand was first established by Robert McNish in 1863, the early days of whisky-blending. It is presently available as both a standard blend and a twelve-year-old, and is marketed in a unique seventeenth-century style bottle. As well as Grand MacNish, Macduff's product range includes the Islay Mist deluxe blend and Lauders, one of the oldest blends on the market.

TYPE
Blend

STRENGTH
43%

TASTE RATING
2

MINIATURES
Yes

VISITORS

A nicely balanced whisky with a fragrant aroma, Haig is smooth and easy to drink, with a long, sweet finish.

*H*aig is a family name long associated with the whisky industry, going back almost 350 years, when Robert Haig, a farmer of Stirlingshire, was rebuked by his local kirk session for distilling his whisky on a Sunday. The family had connections by marriage to the Steins, another of the big Lowland distilling families, and the Jamesons, the Dublin whiskey distillers. The Haigs were instrumental in introducing new practices and machinery (for example, the new patent still in the 1830s) to the grain distilleries which they built in Edinburgh and the east. The company was acquired by the Distillers Company in 1919 and is now owned by United Distillers.

Heather Cream

Inver House Distillers,
Moffat Distillery,
Airdrie, Lanarkshire

TYPE

Cream liqueur

STRENGTH

17%

TASTE RATING

2

MINIATURES

Yes

COMMENTS

Heather Cream is a sweet blend of cream and malt whisky, and is one of the most popular of the Scotch whisky cream liqueurs available today.

VISITORS

The distillery and plant are not open to visitors.

*H*eather Cream's producers, Inver House Distillers, also produce Pinwinnie de luxe blend, among others. They are owners of Knockdhu (producing An Cnoc single malt) and Speyburn-Glenlivet distilleries, and have recently added to their complement of malt distilleries by buying Pultney and Balblair from Allied Distillers. Heather Cream is produced at their complex at Moffat Distillery on the outskirts of Airdrie; a converted former paper mill, it is also home to a grain distillery.

Highland Park

*Highland Park Distillery,
Kirkwall, Orkney*

TYPE
Single malt

BOTTLING AGE
12 years

STRENGTH
40%

TASTE RATING
3–4

MINIATURES
Yes

COMMENTS

Highland Park is a medium-bodied single malt of character, with a heathery–smoky aroma and peaty flavour with balancing sweet tones.

VISITORS

Visitors are welcome 1000–1700 Mon.–Fri., Apr.–Oct., and 1200–1700 Sat. & Sun., Jul.–Aug. Large groups should book in advance. Telephone 01856-874619 to arrange, and for details of winter opening.

*H*ighland Park's origins are linked with an illegal bothy which previously occupied the site. Its owner was one of whisky's most colourful characters, Magnus Eunson. A United Presbyterian church elder by day and smuggler by night, his piety did not prevent his using the church pulpit as a handy hiding place for his illicit distillations. The distillery was founded in 1798 and passed to the Grant family in 1895. Highland Distilleries purchased it in 1937. The different nature of Orcadian peat is said to be a factor in the quite distinctive qualities of the islands' whiskies. Highland Park is the more widely available of the islands' two malts.

Immortal Memory

Gordon and MacPhail,
Elgin, Moray

Immortal memory

Scotch Whisky

RARE SELECTED

Distilled, Blended and Bottled
in Scotland

GORDON & MACPHAIL, ELGIN, SCOTLAND

40% vol   70cl

TYPE

Blend

BOTTLING AGE

8 years

STRENGTH

40%

TASTE RATING

2

MINIATURES

Yes

COMMENTS

A blend which is floral on the nose – perhaps with a hint of parma violets – with a nutty flavour and a warming finish.

VISITORS

Gordon and MacPhail's shop, South St, Elgin is open 0900–1715 Mon.–Wed. (0900–1300 Wed. in winter), 0830–1715 Thu.–Fri., 0900–1700 Sat.

*G*ordon and MacPhail started in business in 1895 as a licensed grocers and wine and spirit merchant, as had done so many of the foremost names among the Scotch whisky blending industry. Unlike the others, however, Gordon and MacPhail have retained all the original aspects of their business as well as extending into vatting, blending and bottling. This blend was declared 'Best Blended Whisky in the World' at the 1991 International Wine and Spirit Competition.

Imperial

Imperial Distillery, Carron, Moray

40% vol. *Product of Scotland* **70** d.

IMPERIAL

TRADEMARK OF PROPRIETORS: ALLIED DISTILLERS LTD

Single Highland Malt

Scotch DISTILLED **1979** *Whisky*

IMPERIAL

Built in 1897, the year of
Queen Victoria's Diamond
Jubilee, the Imperial
Distillery stands
majestically among the
dark woods of Carron,
in a fold of the hills
which encompass the
glittering Spey.

Specially selected,
produced and bottled by
and under the
responsibility of
Gordon & Macphail,
Elgin, Scotland.
Regd. Bottler.

TYPE

Single malt

BOTTLING AGE

Varies

STRENGTH

Varies

TASTE RATING

4

MINIATURES

Yes

COMMENTS

A full-bodied malt with bags of character, Imperial contrives to balance a rich sweetness with a lingering smokiness. Available from independent merchants.

VISITORS

The distillery has no reception centre but visitors are welcome by appointment. Telephone 01340-810276 to arrange.

The patriotically named Imperial Distillery was first established in 1897, the year of Queen Victoria's Diamond Jubilee. Its founder was Thomas Mackenzie, who was already the owner of Dailuaine and Talisker distilleries. All three were brought together under the name of Dailuaine-Talisker Distilleries Ltd. Imperial Distillery was modernized in the mid 1950s. Production was halted temporarily in the 1980s, but was restarted again after Imperial's purchase by Allied Distillers in 1988, and its production now goes into their blends.

Inchgower

*Inchgower Distillery,
Buckie, Banffshire*

TYPE

Single malt

BOTTLING AGE

14 years

STRENGTH

43%

TASTE RATING

2–3

MINIATURES

Yes

COMMENTS

A robust, distinctly heavy-bodied malt with a combination of nutty, fruity and spicy aromas, and a hint of sweetness in its tones.

VISITORS

Visitors are welcome by appointment. Telephone 01542-831161.·

*I*nchgower Distillery was moved from Tochineal by its founder, Alexander Wilson, to its present site at Rathaven near Buckie, to take advantage of the ready supply of water from the Letter Burn and the Springs of Aultmoor. When the original firm went out of business, the distillery passed to Buckie Town Council who sold it to Arthur Bell & Sons for £1000 in 1938. Most of the whisky goes into Bell's blends and the distillery is now owned by United Distillers. The single malt is still relatively rare, only becoming available in official bottlings in the Distillery (Flora and Fauna) Malts series early in the 1990s.

Inchmurrin

Loch Lomond Distillery,
Alexandria, Dunbartonshire

TYPE
Single malt

BOTTLING AGE
10 years

STRENGTH
40%

TASTE RATING
2

MINIATURES
Yes

COMMENTS

A clean, light, pre-dinner malt with a fresh, floral note. A Highland malt with a Lowland character.

VISITORS

The distillery is not open to visitors.

A relatively recent addition to the ranks of Scotland's distilleries, Loch Lomond distillery was founded in 1966 on the site of an old printing and bleaching plant. Like Glengoyne, it just qualifies as being a Highland malt and is situated just to the south of the famous loch. A grain distillery now shares the site. Its present owners, Loch Lomond Distillery Co., recently took control of two more malt distilleries, Littlemill at Bowling and Glen Scotia in Campbeltown, both of which are currently moth-balled.

Invergordon

Invergordon Distillery,
Invergordon, Ross-shire

TYPE

Grain

BOTTLING AGE

10 years

STRENGTH

40%

TASTE RATING

1

MINIATURES

Yes

COMMENTS

A light, clean, smooth whisky with a gentle, slightly vanilla-like taste.

VISITORS

The distillery is not open to visitors.

*B*uilt in the late 1950s to provide work in an area of high unemployment, Invergordon grain distillery is now one of the biggest distilleries in Europe. Like other distilleries in the area, a provost of Inverness had a hand in its establishment. Along with the seven former Invergordon Distillers' malt distilleries, this giant grain complex was acquired in 1993 by Whyte & Mackay. Ben Wyvis malt distillery was added on the same site but is now closed.

Inverleven

*Inverleven Distillery,
Dumbarton, Dunbartonshire*

TYPE
Single malt

BOTTLING AGE
Varies

STRENGTH
Varies

TASTE RATING
2

MINIATURES
Yes

COMMENTS
A relatively smooth Lowland malt, with a nice balance of dry and sweet flavours. Available from independent whisky merchants only.

VISITORS
The distillery is not suitable for visitors.

*B*uilt in 1938, Inverleven is part of a modern-looking, multi-storey red-brick plant, which includes Dumbarton grain distillery, on the banks of the Leven in Dumbarton. It stands on the Highland Line (the line initiated by the Customs and Excise to differentiate area boundaries between styles of whisky), and is classified as a Lowland distillery. It is owned by Allied Distillers and almost all of its output goes into their blends, which include the popular Ballantine's, Teacher's and Long John blends.

Island Prince

*Isle of Arran Distillers Ltd,
Mauchline, Ayrshire*

TYPE
Blend

STRENGTH
40%

TASTE RATING
2-3

MINIATURES
Yes

COMMENTS
A very smooth blend of very old malt and grains, the youngest of which is 21 years old, this has a delicate, slight sweet aroma with peaty notes coming through on the finish.

*I*sle of Arran Distillers are a dynamic new player in the Scotch whisky industry. Independent and family-run, the company has a portfolio of blended and malt whiskies which has been successfully marketed throughout Europe, the Americas and Asia. In 1995, the company opened a new distillery on Arran at Lochranza and its first produce is presently maturing, with an expected launch as a single malt early in the new millenium.

Islay Mist

*MacDuff International,
Glasgow*

TYPE

De luxe

BOTTLING AGE

8, 12, 17 years

STRENGTH

40%, 43%

TASTE RATING

3

MINIATURES

Yes

COMMENTS

*T*he blenders of Islay Mist, MacDuff International, are an independent Scotch whisky company. This mellow Islay de luxe blend made its first appearance in 1928 to mark the twenty-first birthday of Lord Margadale. As well as Islay Mist, their product range includes Lauder's, one of the oldest blends in the Scotch whisky market, as well as Grand MacNish and Strathbeag blends.

This de luxe blend instantly betrays its origins, though as the name suggests, it is mellower in taste than its main component, Laphroaig. Islay Mist is matured in oak casks and is ideal as an introduction for those wishing to sample the delights of the Islay whiskies.

VISITORS

The blending and bottling plant is not open to visitors.

Isle of Jura

*Isle of Jura Distillery,
Craighouse, Jura, Argyllshire*

TYPE

Single malt

BOTTLING AGE

10 years

STRENGTH

40%, 43%

TASTE RATING

3

MINIATURES

Yes

COMMENTS

Reminiscent of a Highland malt, though with a light, clean, fragrant palate of its own, this Island malt is ideal as an aperitif.

VISITORS

Visitors are welcome by appointment. Telephone 01496-820240 to arrange.

*T*he distillery is one of the main employers on this island of around 200 inhabitants. It was first built overlooking the Sound of Jura in 1810, next to a cave where illicit distillation may have been carried on for as long as three centuries. The distillery's machinery and buildings were owned by different individuals, and a dispute between the two led to its closure for over fifty years in 1913. It was effectively redesigned and rebuilt before its reopening in the 1960s. The present owners are Whyte & Mackay who acquired it, and six other malt distilleries, after their purchase of Invergordon Distillers in 1993.

RARE

A BLEND OF THE PUREST OLD SCOTCH WHISKIES

J&B

JUSTERINI & BROOKS
St. James... London 17

KING GEORGE III   KING EDWARD VII
KING WILLIAM IV   KING GEORGE V
QUEEN VICTORIA   KING GEORGE VI

AND TO HIS LATE ROYAL HIGHNESS
THE PRINCE OF WALES (1921-1936)

PRODUCT OF SCOTLAND

70cl e   40% vol.

J & B Rare

*Justerini and Brooks,
London*

TYPE	
Blend	
STRENGTH	
40%, 43%	
TASTE RATING	
2	
MINIATURES	
Yes	
COMMENTS	

J & B Rare is a smooth, sweet-tasting whisky with a light, fresh character. It is the second-best selling Scotch whisky in the world.

Justerini and Brooks' principal founder, Giacomo Justerini, was a wine merchant from Bologna who was infatuated by an Italian opera singer, whom he followed to London in the mid-eighteenth century. There he set up the wine merchants, Justerini & Brooks. In 1962 the company amalgamated with four others to form International Distillers and Vintners Ltd (IDV). Grand Metropolitan bought IDV, then part of Watney Mann & Truman, in 1972. As well as the very popular J & B Rare, the number two whisky worldwide, the company also produces J & B Reserve, a more mature fifteen-year-old blend, J & B Jet, a twelve-year-old de luxe whisky, and J & B Ultima, a fine blend containing no less than 128 whiskies which was launched in 1994.

J & B Jet

*Justerini & Brooks,
London*

TYPE
Blend

STRENGTH
43%

TASTE RATING
3

MINIATURES
No

COMMENTS
Jet has has fresh, fragrant aroma which leads into a rich, mellow taste with unexpected sweet notes.

$\mathcal{J}$ usterini & Brooks' principal founder, Giacomo Justerini, was a wine merchant from Bologna who was infatuated by an Italian opera singer, whom he followed to London in the mid-eighteenth century. He set up the wine merchants, Justerini and Brooks in the capital in 1749 and began selling Scotch thirty years later. In 1962 the company built on previous amalgamations by combining with W. & A. Gilbey to form International Distillers and Vintners Ltd (IDV). Grand Metropolitan bought IDV, then part of Watney Mann & Truman, in 1972. Jet took J&B twelve years to develop as a major product in the premium Scotch market. A high proportion of Speyside malts is used in its blend of twelve- and fifteen-year-old whiskies.

Johnnie Walker
Black Label

United Distillers,
Kilmarnock, Ayrshire

Johnnie Walker.
BLACK LABEL
Old Scotch Whisky

TYPE

De luxe

BOTTLING AGE

12 years

STRENGTH

43%

TASTE RATING

2–3

MINIATURES

Yes

COMMENTS

*I*n common with other entrepreneurs who became the major operators in the whisky-blending industry, the original Johnnie Walker began as a licensed grocer in Kilmarnock in 1820. It was his grandsons who created the Black Label and Red Label blends in the early 1900s. His son, Alexander Walker, bought Cardow Distillery in 1893, thus ensuring a regular supply of malt for their blends. In 1925 the company joined the Distillers Company Ltd who bought the Talisker and Dailuaine distilleries and licensed the former to Walker. Johnnie Walker Black Label is now owned by United Distillers.

The best-selling de luxe Scotch whisky in the world, it has a special quality of smoothness and a depth of taste and character which linger on the palate.

Johnnie Walker
Blue Label

United Distillers,
Kilmarnock, Ayrshire

TYPE

Blend

STRENGTH

43%

STRENGTH

2–3

MINIATURES

No

COMMENTS

Blue Label is among the most exclusive of blended whiskies, with a subtle and complex character and a rich, pleasing flavour.

*I*ntroduced to the UK market in 1992 under its new name, Blue Label is the latest and most up-market addition to the family of Johnnie Walker 'coloured label' whiskies. Most of the product is intended to go for export, particularly to Japanese markets. The Johnnie Walker company began as a family-run licensed grocers in Kilmarnock in 1820 and by the end of the century had become one of the major players in the Scotch industry. It was a Walker's employee, James Stevenson, who was instrumental in persuading the government to introduce a minimum period of maturation in bond for whisky, in the process raising quality standards and doing the industry a major service. Johnnie Walker is now one of United Distillers' major blending names.

Johnnie Walker Red Label

United Distillers, Kilmarnock, Ayrshire

TYPE

Blend

STRENGTH

43%

TASTE RATING

2

MINIATURES

Yes

COMMENTS

A smooth blend with sweet and dry notes of maltiness and peatiness. Red Label is the world's biggest-selling blended whisky.

*I*n common with other entrepreneurs who became the major operators in the whisky-blending industry, the original Johnnie Walker began as a licensed grocer in Kilmarnock in 1820. It was his grandsons who created the Black Label and Red Label blends in the early 1900s. His son, Alexander Walker, bought Cardow Distillery in 1893, thus ensuring a regular supply of malt for their blends. In 1925 the company joined the Distillers Company Ltd who bought the Talisker and Dailuaine distilleries and licensed the former to Walker. Johnnie Walker Red Label is now owned by United Distillers.

Knockando

*Knockando Distillery,
Knockando, Aberlour,
Banffshire*

TYPE
Single malt

BOTTLING AGE
Bottled when ready, rather than at a set age; always at least twelve years.

STRENGTH
40%, 43%

TASTE RATING
3–4

MINIATURES
Yes

COMMENTS
Knockando is a light, easy-to-drink single malt, with pleasantly smooth, nutty hints.

VISITORS
Visitors are welcome by appointment. Telephone 01340-6205 to arrange.

*B*uilt during the 1890s whisky boom, Knockando is today owned by International Distillers and Vintners. The distillery's name is said to mean 'small black hill', and Knockando itself is set on a hill overlooking the Spey. Knockando single malt is bottled only when it is considered to have reached its peak rather than at a pre-determined age – generally, this is between twelve and fifteen years. The label lists the year of distillation – the 'season' – and the year of bottling. Such season dating recalls the time when Scottish distilleries only distilled during the winter season after the barley harvest.

162

Lagavulin

*Lagavulin Distillery,
Port Ellen, Islay, Argyllshire*

TYPE
Single malt

BOTTLING AGE
16 years

STRENGTH
43%

TASTE RATING
5

MINIATURES
Yes

COMMENTS
A distinctively Islay malt, powerful and demanding, with a dominant aroma and a dry, peaty–smoky flavour complemented by a trace of sweetness.

VISITORS
Visitors are welcome by appointment. Telephone 01496-302400 to arrange.

*D*istilling was carried on in this area from the 1740s, when moonshiners made and smuggled illicit whisky to the mainland. Lagavulin's own history is entangled with these times, although the distillery dates officially from the 1810s. Peter Mackie, the main driving force behind the success of White Horse, started out on his distilling career at Lagavulin, and its produce was later to feature strongly in his blend. Lagavulin went into partnership with Mackie's company, subsequently the White Horse Company, and the whisky is still used in White Horse blends today. The distillery is owned by United Distillers.

Laphroaig

Laphroaig Distillery,
Port Ellen, Islay, Argyllshire

TYPE
Single malt

BOTTLING AGE
10, 15 years

STRENGTH
40%, 43%, up to 45.1%

TASTE RATING
5

MINIATURES
Yes

COMMENTS
A robust, full-bodied, classic Islay malt with a trace of seaweed in its strongly peaty flavour.

VISITORS
Visitors are welcome by appointment, Sept.–end June. Telephone 01496-302418 to arrange.

LAPHROAIG®

SINGLE ISLAY MALT
SCOTCH WHISKY

10
Years Old

The most richly flavoured of
all Scotch whiskies
ESTABLISHED
1815

D. JOHNSTON & CO. (LAPHROAIG), LAPHROAIG DISTILLERY, ISLE OF ISLAY

40%vol   IMPORTADOR WENCESLAO PAZ MARTINEZ
DOMICILIO C HADOU S/N R.E. NUM 40.1.125 ML   70cl

Laphroaig Distillery is set on a bay on Islay's southern shore, and dates back to 1815. It is a traditional distillery and one of the few still to have a hand-turned malting floor, ensuring the traditional taste. It is owned by Allied Distillers, who consider the single malt, a top-five seller in the UK malts list and one of the top ten around the world, to be the star performer across their entire portfolio. Laphroaig is also one of the components in their Long John, Ballantine's and Teacher's blends, as well as in the quality Black Bottle blend, which Allied recently sold to Matthew Gloag & Son, blenders of The Famous Grouse.

70 cl 40%vol

PRODUCT OF SCOTLAND

ESTD 1834

LAUDER'S®
SCOTCH

Blended Scotch Whisky

BLENDED AND SHIPPED BY

Archibald Lauder & Co Ltd.

GLASGOW, SCOTLAND

DISTILLÉ ET MIS EN BOUTEILLE EN ÉCOSSE
IMPORTÉ PAR SAR. J. NOUY, GUADELOUPE

DISTILLED AND BOTTLED IN SCOTLAND
UNDER BRITISH GOVERNMENT SUPERVISION

Lauder's Scotch

*Macduff International,
Glasgow*

TYPE
Blend

STRENGTH
40% and 43%

TASTE RATING
2

MINIATURES
Yes

COMMENTS
A smooth, nicely rounded and easy-to-drink blend.

VISITORS
The blending and bottling plant is not open to visitors.

The blenders of Lauders, Macduff International, are an independent Scotch whisky company. Lauders has been in continuous production since 1836, making it one of the oldest brands available on the market. Throughout its long history, Lauders has won several gold medals in competition both at thome and overseas. As well as Lauders, Macduff International's product range includes the Islay Mist de luxe, as well as the Grand MacNish and Stewart Macduff blends.

Ledaig

Tobermory Distillery, Tobermory, Mull, Argyllshire

LEDAIG

SINGLE MALT
FROM
THE ISLE OF MULL

1974
Vintage

*This rare old single malt whisky
was distilled at the Ledaig Distillery
on the Isle of Mull by
Ledaig Distillers (Tobermory) Ltd.*

PRODUCE OF SCOTLAND

70cl Sole agent for Switzerland
Jacques Vins et Spiritueux
Jacques Szmulovski Geneve. 43%Vol

TYPE
Single malt

BOTTLING AGE
20, 21 years

STRENGTH
43%

TASTE RATING
5

MINIATURES
No

COMMENTS
A full-bodied single malt from the Tobermory Distillery, Ledaig has strongly peaty flavours.

VISITORS
The Visitor Centre and Distillery Shop are open Mon.–Fri., Easter–30 Sept. Tours can be arranged at other times in the year. Telephone 01688-302645.

Set in a wooded site by the sea, Tobermory Distillery has enjoyed mixed fortunes since it was first established in 1823. It has been closed several times during its existence, most recently in the 1980s when it was mothballed. Having reopened in 1990, Tobermory is now back in production and it remains one of the few family-owned independent whisky distilleries. The distillery was previously known as Ledaig, changing its name in the 1970s. A single malt is also available under the distillery's new name of Tobermory.

Linkwood

*Linwood Distillery,
Elgin, Moray*

TYPE
Single malt

BOTTLING AGE
12 years

STRENGTH
43%

TASTE RATING
4–5

MINIATURES
Yes

COMMENTS
Linkwood is widely acclaimed as one of the best Speyside malts, having the area's characteristics in a fine balance: smoky, and with a fruity sweetness underlying its malty tones.

VISITORS
Visitors are welcome by appointment, 0800–1630. Telephone 01343-547004.

*T*his is one of the most traditional of distilleries despite extensive rebuilding work carried out three times since its establishment in the 1820s: it is said that equipment was never replaced until absolutely necessary, and even a spider's web was not removed in case the change of environment would affect the whisky. Built by a former provost of Elgin, Linkwood has an attractive wooded setting by Linkwood Burn outside the town. The distillery is owned by United Distillers.

Littlemill

Littlemill Distillery,
Bowling, Dunbartonshire

TYPE
Single malt

BOTTLING AGE
8 years

STRENGTH
40%

TASTE RATING
2–3

MINIATURES
Yes

COMMENTS
A light Lowland malt with a smooth, sweet flavour. Good as an aperitif.

VISITORS
The distillery is not open to the public.

Littlemill began life as a brewery centuries before distilling was started, with its ale apparently crossing the Clyde to supply the monks of Paisley Abbey. It was established as a distillery in the late eighteenth century and is one of the oldest in Scotland. Its water comes from the Kilpatrick Hills, to the north of the Highland Line (the line initiated by the Customs and Excise to differentiate the area boundaries between different styles of whisky), although Littlemill is a Lowland distillery and whisky. Owned until 1994 by Gibson International, it is now, with its sister distillery of Glen Scotia, under the control of the Loch Lomond Distillery Co., the producers of Inchmurrin single malt. Both Littlemill and Glen Scotia are presently mothballed.

The Loch Fyne

Loch Fyne Whiskies, Inveraray, Argyll

TYPE
Blend

STRENGTH
40%

TASTE RATING
2–3

MINIATURES
Yes

COMMENTS
A malt drinker's blend, full flavoured, with a raisiny, sweet spiced nose, mellow smoothness of taste and a warmng finish. A very easy-to-drink whisky.

VISITORS
The shop is open all year, 1000–1730 (except Sun., Nov.–Mar.). Telephone 01499-302219 for mail-order information.

*L*och Fyne Whiskies is an independent specialist shop devoted to selling only whisky and whisky-related products. First registered in 1884, the current Loch Fyne blend was created by Ronnie Martin, a former production director of DCL/United Distillers. His mastery of blending was recognised when in 1996, The Loch Fyne won the bronze award in the influential International Wine & Spirit Competition. Produced in small quantities, The Loch Fyne is available only in Argyll or by mail-order. (Postal customers also receive a copy of the company's informed, witty and enthusiastic biannual newsletter, *Scotch Whisky Review*.)

Loch Ranza

*Isle of ArranDistillers Ltd,
Mauchline, Ayrshire*

TYPE
Blend

STRENGTH
40%

TASTE RATING
2

MINIATURES
Yes

COMMENTS
Named after the home of the new Isle of Arran distillery, this is a very smooth, slightly sweet dram which is ideal as a pre-dinner dram.

*I*sle of Arran Distillers are a dynamic new player in the Scotch whisky industry. Independent and family-run, the company has a portfolio of blended and malt whiskies which has been successfully marketed throughout Europe, the Americas and Asia. In 1995, the company opened a new distillery on Arran at Lochranza and its first produce is presently maturing, with an expected launch as a single malt early in the new millenium.

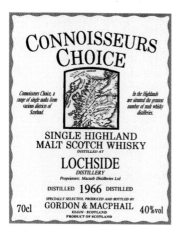

CONNOISSEURS CHOICE

Connoisseurs Choice, a range of single malts from various districts of Scotland

In the Highlands are situated the greatest number of malt whisky distilleries.

SINGLE HIGHLAND MALT SCOTCH WHISKY
DISTILLED AT
LOCHSIDE
DISTILLERY
Proprietors: Macnab Distilleries Ltd

DISTILLED **1966** DISTILLED

70cl

SPECIALLY SELECTED, PRODUCED AND BOTTLED BY
GORDON & MACPHAIL
ELGIN · SCOTLAND
PRODUCT OF SCOTLAND

40%vol

Lochside

*Lochside Distillery,
Montrose, Angus*

TYPE
Single malt

BOTTLING AGE
10 years

STRENGTH
40%

TASTE RATING
2

MINIATURES
No

COMMENTS

A light-to-medium-bodied single malt with a sweet, fruity aroma and drier, smooth flavour. It is difficult to find under the distillery label, but supplies will continue to be available from independent merchants.

*E*stablished as recently as 1957, Lochside has been one of the shorter-lived Scotch whisky distilleries. It was built on the site of an eighteenth-century brewery and originally comprised two distilleries, one grain and one malt, as well as a blending plant. The distillery closed its grain-distilling and blending facilities in the late 1970s and continued in malt production only until 1992, when it was shut down completely by its Spanish owners.

Long John

*Allied Distillers,
Dumbarton, Dumbartonshire*

TYPE
Blend

STRENGTH
40%, 43%

TASTE RATING
2–3

MINIATURES
Yes

COMMENTS
A medium-bodied blend with a very slight peaty tang to its pleasant, nicely rounded flavour.

VISITORS
The plant is not suitable for visitors.

*T*he original company was founded by 'Long' John Macdonald, a statuesque man who built Ben Nevis Distillery at Fort William in 1825. The distillery had grain and malt stills, and its produce changed from a malt to a blend around the turn of the century. The Long John company name and the distillery went separate ways, and the company was bought by Chaplin, a London wine and spirit merchant in 1911. They in turn were acquired by the spirit merchants Seager, Evans in 1936. The company changed its name to Long John International in 1971 and, after several acquisitions, it is now operated by Allied Distillers.

Longmorn

*Longmorn Distillery,
Elgin, Moray*

TYPE
Single malt

BOTTLING AGE
12, 15 years

STRENGTH
40%, 43%, 45%

TASTE RATING
3–4

MINIATURES
Yes

COMMENTS
Another classic Speyside malt of great character, Longmorn is a full-bodied whisky with a clean, fragrant aroma and a nutty, sweet taste.

VISITORS
The distillery is not open to visitors.

*T*he distillery was built by John Duff in 1894 and stands on the road between Elgin and Rothes. Nearby is an old water wheel dating from the seventeenth century, although the distillery draws its water from a local spring. Longmorn, along with its sister distillery of Benriach, merged with The Glenlivet and Glen Grant Distilleries and Hill Thomson to form The Glenlivet Distillers. The distillery at that time was known as Longmorn-Glenlivet, but has now dropped its hyphenated suffix. The company was purchased by Seagram in 1976.

Longrow

Springbank Distillery,
Campbelltown, Argyllshire

TYPE
Single malt

BOTTLING AGE
21 years

STRENGTH
46%

TASTE RATING
5

MINIATURES
Yes

COMMENTS
Longrow is a pungent malt whose production process, using only peat-dried barley, lends it a distinctive, peaty taste with an almost medicinal aroma, yet a complementary trace of sweetness.

VISITORS
Springbank Distillery is open to visitors strictly by appointment. Telephone 01586-552085 to arrange.

Springbank Distillery produces Longrow as its second malt. It is called after another Campbeltown distillery of that name, which was closed in the late 1800s. The Longrown malt is so strongly peated that it has often been likened to an Islay malt. Springbank is a one-off among Scots distilleries for several reasons:it is the only distillery-label malt which follows traditional techniques of not chill-filtering; it is the only distillery to carry out all production techniques, from floor malting to bottling; it is the only distillery in Campbeltown not to have closed; and it has been owned by the same family for close on two centuries.

The Macallan

Macallan Distillery, Craigellachie, Banffshire

TYPE
Single malt

BOTTLING AGE
7, 10, 12, 18, 25 years

STRENGTH
40%, 43%, 57%

TASTE RATING
3–4

MINIATURES
Yes

COMMENTS
Its rich, sherried aroma with a hint of peaches, its smooth, elegant flavour and its delightfully mellow aftertaste make the Macallan one of the most popular of malts

VISITORS
Visitors are welcome by appointment on weekdays. Telephone 01340-871471.

The Macallan's distinctive richness of taste and colour derives in part from its ageing in sweet sherry casks, a traditional practice which this distillery is the only one to maintain through all its range. The distillery itself originated on a farm set above a ford over the River Spey which was used by drovers travelling south. Distilling was probably under way on this site in the 1700s with the first licensed distilling taking place around 1824. It was bought and extended in 1892 by Richard Kemp, whose descendants owned the company until it was acquired by Highland Distilleries in 1996. The whisky has been one of the best selling malts for ten years.

Stewart Macduff

Macduff International, Glasgow

TYPE
Blend

STRENGTH
40%, 43%

TASTE RATING
2

MINIATURES
Yes

COMMENTS
A smooth, medium-bodied blend of Highland, Islay and Lowland malts with mildly peaty overtones.

VISITORS
The blending and bottling plant is not open to visitors.

Stewart Macduff is a relative newcomer to the range of whiskies produced by Macduff International Ltd, an independent Scotch whisky company. As well as this blend, the company's portfolio includes the de luxe Islay Mist blend and Lauders, one of the oldest brands of Scotch on the market, as well as the Grand MacNish and Strathbeag blends.

Millburn

Millburn Distillery,
Inverness, Inverness-shire

TYPE
Single malt

BOTTLING AGE
Varies

STRENGTH
Varies

TASTE RATING
3–4

MINIATURES
Yes

COMMENTS
A rich Highland malt of medium-to-full body with a certain fruitiness in the palate and a balancing dry finish. Available from independent merchants.

Millburn was one of three Inverness distilleries (the others being Glen Albyn and Glen Mhor), none of which is still in existence, Millburn itself having been closed in 1985 and later sold off by its owners, United Distillers. It was also one of the older Highland distilleries, having been established around 1825, although distilling was said to have been carried out on the site as early as 1807. All its produce was traditionally used for blending, so it is difficult to find as a single and its malt will, of course, become rarer in future.

Miltonduff

*Miltonduff-Glenlivet
Distillery, Elgin, Moray*

TYPE
Single malt

BOTTLING AGE
12 years

STRENGTH
40%, 43%

TASTE RATING
2–3

MINIATURES
No

COMMENTS
A nice Speyside malt, medium-bodied and smooth, with a floral note.

VISITORS
Visitors are welcome by appointment. Telephone 01343-547433 to arrange.

*M*iltonduff-Glenlivet Distillery stands just to the south of Elgin near Pluscarden Abbey; the distillery's old mashhouse was said to have been built on the site of the abbey's brewery. The distillery itself was founded in 1824, and draws its water from the nearby Black Burn which flows down peaty Black Hill. Miltonduff was one of the original Hiram Walker distilleries acquired in 1937 and today is operated by Allied Distillers who use it in their blends, notably Ballantine's, and market the single particularly through duty-free outlets.

Mortlach

Mortlach Distillery,
Dufftown, Keith, Banffshire

SPEYSIDE SINGLE MALT SCOTCH WHISKY

MORTLACH

was the first of seven
distilleries in Dufftown. In the
old farm animals kept in
adjoining byres were fed on
barley left over from processing
Today water from springs in
the CONVAL HILLS is used to
produce this delightful
smooth, fruity single
MALT SCOTCH WHISKY.

AGED **16** YEARS

Distilled & Bottled at MORTLACH
Mortlach's Distillery
Dufftown, Keith, Banffshire, Scotland

43% vol   70 cl

TYPE
Single malt

BOTTLING AGE
16 years

STRENGTH
43%

TASTE RATING
4

MINIATURES
Yes

COMMENTS
A Speyside malt of mellow, fruity flavour with a definite peatiness and a dryness in the finish.

VISITORS
Visitors are welcome by appointment. Telephone 01340-820318 to arrange.

Another of Dufftown's distilleries, this time standing in a little valley outside the town, by the River Dullan. The distillery draws its water not from the river but from springs in the local Conval Hills. Founded in 1823, it was, in fact, the first of the distilleries to be built in the capital of Speyside whisky-making, and it enjoyed a monopoly in the town until 1887. The distillery has been modernized twice this century and is now owned by United Distillers, who did not officially bottle its malt until it featured in the Distillery (Flora and Fauna) Malts series in the 1990s.

North Port

*North Port Distillery,
Brechin, Angus*

TYPE
Single malt

BOTTLING AGE
Varies

STRENGTH
Varies

TASTE RATING
2

MINIATURES
Yes

COMMENTS
Available from independent bottling merchants, North Port is a light-bodied, dry, fairly astringent whisky, best drunk as an aperitif.

*T*he older of the two distilleries in Brechin (Glencadam being the other), North Port was founded in 1820 by David Guthrie, a prominent Brechin businessman and local politician and managed by his sons from 1823; two brothers in the Guthrie family had interests in the whisky industry while a third, Thomas, was active in the temperance movement. The distillery, latterly owned by the Distillers Company Ltd, was closed down in 1983 and sold in 1990.

Oban

Oban Distillery,
Oban, Argyllshire

TYPE
Single malt

BOTTLING AGE
14 years

STRENGTH
43%

TASTE RATING
2–3

MINIATURES
Yes

COMMENTS
An intriguing, complex malt with a full Island character which is balanced by a soft Highland finish.

VISITORS
Visitors are welcome 0930–1700 Mon.–Fri. all year and 0930– 1700 Sat., Easter–Oct. Telephone 01631-62110.

*F*irst built as a brewery in 1794, Oban Distillery was part of the grand plan of the Stevensons, a family of energetic entrepreneurs and the founders of modern Oban at that time. The distillery, a grey building standing on the harbour front, draws its water from the Ardconnel area of peaty hills a mile from the town. It is licensed to John Hopkins, now owned by United Distillers, who currently feature the single in their Classic Malts series.

Old Fettercairn

Fettercairn Distillery,
Fettercairn, Laurencekirk
Kincardineshire

TYPE
Single malt

BOTTLING AGE
10 years

STRENGTH
40%, 43%

TASTE RATING
3–4

MINIATURES
Yes

COMMENTS
A smooth single malt with a full, malty taste and a satisfyingly dry counterbalance.

VISITORS
Visitors are welcome at the distillery's visitor centre 1000–1630 Mon.–Sat., May–Sept. Telephone 01561-340205 to arrange group bookings.

*F*irst established at its present location in 1824 by Sir Alexander Ramsay, Fettercairn is one of the country's oldest distilleries. Despite its age, it proved receptive to modern production methods when it became the first distillery in the country to use oil for heating its stills. It was once owned by John Gladstone, the father of the great Victorian prime minister W. E. Gladstone. Fettercairn is situated on the fringes of the Grampian Mountains, from which it takes its spring-water supplies. The distillery, which was extended in 1966, is presently owned by Whyte & Mackay.

Old Parr

United Distillers,
Banbeath, Leven, Fife

TYPE	
De luxe	
BOTTLING AGE	
12 years	
STRENGTH	
43%	
TASTE RATING	
2	
MINIATURES	
No	
COMMENTS	

A blend of fine whiskies, with a smooth and mellow taste and exceptional depth of flavour.

*T*he firm which produced Old Parr, Macdonald Greenlees, is now owned by United Distillers. The brand was first produced in the early twentieth century by the Greenlees brothers from Glasgow, and was aimed specifically at the southern English market. After the First World War, the company amalgamated with Alexander & Macdonald of Leith and William Williams of Aberdeen, owners of Glendullan Distillery. The whole company joined the Distillers Company Ltd in 1925. Old Parr is a major export blend in Central and South American, Japan and the Far Eastern markets.

100 Pipers

Chivas Brothers,
Paisley

TYPE
Blend

STRENGTH
40%

TASTE RATING
2

MINIATURES
Yes

COMMENTS
A smooth, mellow blend with a light, smoky finish.

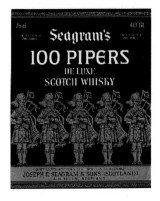

*C*hivas Brothers is a subsidiary of the Canadian drinks firm Seagram, by whom it was bought in 1949. The origins of the Chivas Brothers company can be traced back to the establishment of a wine and spirit merchant and licensed grocer in Aberdeen in 1801. As the owner of nine distilleries, Seagram is an important company in the Scotch whisky market. 100 Pipers is one of several Seagram-owned blended whiskies, among which Passport and the de luxe Chivas Regal and Royal Salute are especially well regarded.

The Original Mackinlay

Invergordon Distillers,
Leith, Edinburgh

TYPE
Blend

STRENGTH
40%

TASTE RATING
2

MINIATURES
Yes

COMMENTS
A well-balanced and nicely aged whisky with a smooth, malty aroma and a relatively full, lingering and slightly sweet flavour.

VISITORS
The blending and bottling plant is not open to visitors.

*T*he success of the Mackinlay firm began under James, son of Charles Mackinlay, founder of the Leith company in 1824. The original Mackinlays blend appeared in 1850, and James was responsible for its success in the lucrative markets of southern England, gaining contracts to supply whisky to the House of Commons and to Ernest Shackleton's 1907 expedition to the South Pole. James Mackinlay was a co-founder of Glen Mhor Distillery, and bought Glen Albyn at the end of the nineteenth century; both were sold in 1972. The company is now owned by Whyte & Mackay. As well as The Original, the Mackinlay range also includes twelve-year-old and twenty-one-year-old blends.

Passport

Chivas Brothers,
Paisley

TYPE
Blend

STRENGTH
40%

TASTE RATING
2-3

MINIATURES
Yes

COMMENTS
A well-rounded blend which has the Glen Keith single malt at its core. Sweet, slighty fruity flavours are complemented by a delicate smoky finish.

Chivas Brothers is a subsidiary of the Canadian drinks firm Seagram, by whom it was bought in 1949. The origins of the Chivas Brothers company can be traced back to the establishment of a wine and spirit merchant and licensed grocer in Aberdeen in 1801. Owning nine malt distilleries, Seagram is an important company in the Scotch whisky market. Passport was launched in 1965 after several years' research to produce a blend that would appeal specifically to a younger, less traditional market.

Pinwinnie

Inver House Distillers,
Moffat Distillery, Airdrie,
Lanarkshire

TYPE
De luxe

STRENGTH
40%

TASTE RATING
2–3

MINIATURES
Yes

COMMENTS
A Lowland de luxe blend, Pinwinnie is a very smooth whisky, with sweet, fragrant notes and a nicely rounded finish.

VISITORS
The distillery and plant are not open to visitors.

*P*inwinnie's producers, Inver House, also own Knockdhu (producing An Cnoc single malt) and Speyburn-Glenlivet distilleries, and have also recently acquired Pultney and Balblair. Since a management buy-out from its parent company, Publicker Distillers, in 1988, Inver House has been one of the few independent, Scottish-owned companies in the whisky industry. Blending is carried out at their complex at Moffat on the outskirts of Airdrie in the central Lowlands, a converted former paper mill which also holds a grain distillery.

Pittyvaich

Pittyvaich-Glenlivet Distillery, Dufftown, Keith, Banffshire

TYPE
Single malt

BOTTLING AGE
12 years

STRENGTH
43%

TASTE RATING
4

MINIATURES
Yes

COMMENTS
Pittyvaich is a Speyside malt with a perfumed fruitiness with a hint of spice and a strong aftertaste.

SPEYSIDE
SINGLE MALT
SCOTCH WHISKY

PITTYVAICH

distillery is situated in the *DULLAN GLEN* on the outskirts of Dufftown, near to the historic *Mortlach Church* which dates back to the (). The distillery draws water from two nearby

springs - *CONVALLEYS* and *BALLIEMORE*. Pittyvaich single *MALT SCOTCH WHISKY* has a *perfumed, fruity* nose and a robust flavour with a *hint of spiciness*.

AGED **12** YEARS

Distilled & Bottled in SCOTLAND
PITTYVAICH DISTILLERY
Dufftown, Keith, Banffshire, Scotland

43% vol 70cl

*I*t was the success of neighbouring Dufftown-Glenlivet and the quality of its water supply, from the local Jock's Well, which encouraged Bell to build the brand-new Pittyvaich-Glenlivet Distillery almost next door, in 1974. Almost all of its product now goes into United Distillers' blends, and the single malt was difficult to find until it was officially bottled by UD as part of their Distillery (Flora and Fauna) Malts series. The distillery has now been closed.

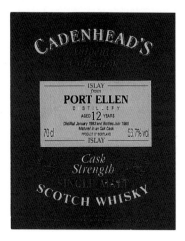

Port Ellen

Port Ellen Distillery,
Port Ellen, Islay, Argyllshire

TYPE
Single malt

BOTTLING AGE
Varies

STRENGTH
Varies

TASTE RATING
3–4

MINIATURES
Yes

COMMENTS
A milder Islay than some, Port Ellen is a basically dry malt with a reasonably mild, smoky and peaty flavour. It is available from independent bottling merchants.

*P*ort Ellen was established in 1824 and stands in the town of the same name in the south of the island. The distillery was closed earlier this century, from 1930 until 1967, when it was re-opened, modernized and enlarged. Its produce has been regarded by some conoisseurs as the classic Islay malt. The distillery, latterly owned by United Distillers, was mothballed in 1984 and has now been closed permanently.

Pride of Islay

Gordon and MacPhail,
Elgin, Moray

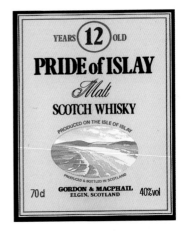

TYPE
Vatted malt

BOTTLING AGE
12 years

STRENGTH
40%

TASTE RATING
4

MINIATURES
Yes

COMMENTS
One of Gordon and MacPhail's series of malts capturing the classic characteristics of the leading regions, this is a vatting of the finest whiskies produced on Islay. It has a complex nose with salty, medicinal and smoky flavours.

VISITORS
Gordon and MacPhail's shop South St, Elgin is open 0900–1715 Mon.–Wed. (0900–1300 Wed. in winter.), 0830–1715 Thu.–Fri., 0900–1700 Sat.

Gordon and MacPhail started in business in 1895 as a licensed grocers and wine and spirit merchant, as had done so many of the foremost names among the Scotch whisky blending industry. Unlike the others, however, Gordon and MacPhail have retained all the original aspects of their business as well as extending into vatting, blending and bottling, and they are today the world's leading malt whisky specialists.

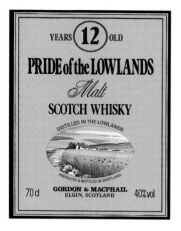

Pride of the Lowlands

Gordon and MacPhail,
Elgin, Moray

TYPE

Vatted malt

BOTTLING AGE

12 years

STRENGTH

40%

TASTE RATING

2

MINIATURES

Yes

COMMENTS

One of Gordon and MacPhail's series of malts capturing the classic characteristics of the leading regions, this is a vatting of the finest whiskies distilled in the Lowlands, and has a sweet, butterscotch-like nose with a smoky–woody finish.

VISITORS

Gordon and MacPhail's shop South St, Elgin is open 0900–1715 Mon.–Wed. (0900–1300 Wed. in winter.), 0830–1715 Thu.–Fri., 0900–1700 Sat.

*G*ordon and MacPhail's premises are located in Elgin on the banks of the River Lossie and close to Speyside, arguably the heart of the Scotch whisky industry. The firm has been in business for almost a century, initially as a licensed grocers and wine and spirit merchants. Their business encompasses the vatting, blending and bottling of whiskies, while their retail shop is among the leading malt whisky shops in the UK.

Pride of Orkney

Gordon and MacPhail,
Elgin, Moray

TYPE
Vatted malt

BOTTLING AGE
12 years

STRENGTH
40%, 43%, 57%

TASTE RATING
3

MINIATURES
Yes

COMMENTS
One of Gordon and MacPhail's series of malts capturing the classic characteristics of the leading regions, this is a vatting of the finest whiskies produced in Orkney, and is a well-balanced whisky with a sweet, toasted nose, with a hint of heather.

VISITORS
Gordon and MacPhail's shop South St, Elgin is open 0900–1715 Mon.–Wed. (0900–1300 Wed. in winter.), 0830–1715 Thu.–Fri., 0900–1700 Sat.

*G*ordon and MacPhail's premises are located in Elgin on the banks of the River Lossie and close to Speyside, arguably the heart of the Scotch whisky industry. The firm has been in business for almost a century, initially as a licensed grocers and wine and spirit merchants. Their business encompasses the vatting, blending and bottling of whiskies, while their retail shop is among the leading malt whisky shops in the UK.

Pride of Strathspey

Gordon and MacPhail,
Elgin, Moray

TYPE
Vatted malt

BOTTLING AGE
12, 25 years

STRENGTH
40%

TASTE RATING
2

MINIATURES
Yes

COMMENTS
One of Gordon and MacPhail's series of malts capturing the classic characteristics of the leading regions, this is a vatting of the finest whiskies distilled in Strathspey. This malt is a citrus-fruity whisky in nose and palate, with a very pleasant aftertaste.

VISITORS
Gordon and MacPhail's shop South St, Elgin is open 0900–1715 Mon.–Wed. (0900–1300 Wed. in winter.), 0830–1715 Thu.–Fri., 0900–1700 Sat.

*G*ordon and MacPhail started in business in 1895 as a licensed grocers and wine and spirit merchant, as had done so many of the foremost names among the Scotch whisky blending industry. Unlike the others, however, Gordon and MacPhail have retained all the original aspects of their business as well as extending into vatting, blending and bottling, and they are today the world's leading malt whisky specialists.

Pulteney

Pulteney Distillery,
Wick, Caithness

TYPE

Single malt

BOTTLING AGE

Varies

STRENGTH

Varies

TASTE RATING

3–4

MINIATURES

Yes

COMMENTS

Reputedly one of the fastest-maturing whiskies, Pulteney is a distinctive malt with a pungent aroma and salty tang underlain by peaty notes, perhaps due to the exposed coastal position of the distillery. Available from independent bottlers.

VISITORS

The distillery is not open to visitors

PURE MALT SCOTCH WHISKY
from
PULTENEY
Distillery

Proprietors: Pulteney Distillery Co. Ltd.

75 cl   Bottled by Wm.Cadenhead,
18 Golden Square, Aberdeen
Scotland   46% vol

*P*ulteney Distillery was established in 1826 in a new district of Wick which had been built to accommodate workers from the local herring industry, and in such a situation it had a ready market. It was closed during the slump of the 1920s and was not reopened until 1951, being sold to James & George Stodart Ltd of Dumbarton, a Hiram Walker subsidiary, four years later. In June 1995 the distillery was sold by Allied Distillers to Inver House Distillers, giving them a complement of four malt distilleries, the others being Knockdhu, Speyburn-Glenlivet and, most recently, Balblair. The most northerly distillery on the Scottish mainland, Pultney is situated near the ruins of the fourteenth-century Castle Oliphant, known as the Auld Man o' Wick.

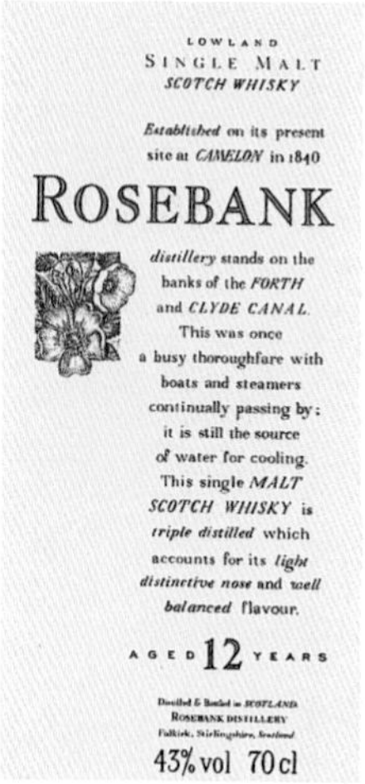

Rosebank

*Rosebank Distillery,
Camelon, Falkirk,
Stirlingshire*

TYPE
Single malt

BOTTLING AGE
12 years

STRENGTH
43%

TASTE RATING
2

MINIATURES
Yes

COMMENTS
One of the best known Lowland malts, Rosebank is a smooth, mild whisky of light and subtle character, which makes it ideal as a pre-dinner dram.

Although a distillery was operating on this site in 1817, the most recent distillery generally dated from 1840, when much rebuilding took place. It stands on the banks of the Forth and Clyde Canal, on the outskirts of Falkirk. Triple distillation processes were used at Rosebank, which had one wash still and two spirit stills. The distillery is now closed. Its single malt was difficult to obtain, although it has been officially bottled in the Distillery (Flora and Fauna) Malts series.

Royal Brackla

*Royal Brackla Distillery,
Cawdor, Nairnshire*

TYPE
Single malt

BOTTLING AGE
10 years

STRENGTH
43%

TASTE RATING
4

MINIATURES
Yes

COMMENTS
A light, fresh, grassy malt with a hint of fruitiness. This single malt can be difficult to find.

VISITORS
Visitors are welcome by appointment. Telephone 016677-404280.

While William IV was known to have enjoyed Brackla's whisky, the distillery has been allowed officially to call itself 'Royal' since 1838, when his neice, the new queen Victoria granted it a Royal Warrant. Founded in 1812, the distillery has been rebuilt and extended several times in the past two centuries, although it is currently mothballed. It is licensed to Bissets, now owned by United Distillers, and almost all of its produce goes into their blends.

Royal Culross

Gibson Scotch Whisky
Distilleries Ltd, Glasgow

TYPE
Vatted malt

BOTTLING AGE
8 years

STRENGTH
43%

TASTE RATING
3–4

MINIATURES
Yes

COMMENTS

Royal Culross is a vatted malt of substantial character and body with a pungent aroma and smooth, malty tones balanced by a lighter, slightly peaty edge.

*R*oyal Culross is one of a range of whiskies, including the popular blend Fraser McDonald and Scotia Royale deluxe blend, which are associated with the Glen Scotia Distillery in Campbeltown. All three are produced by Gibson Scotch Whisky Distilleries Ltd, a subsidiary of the Loch Lomond Distillery Co. Ltd of Alexandria. The company now has three malt distilleries (Loch Lomond which produces Inchmurrin, a Highland malt, Littlemill, a Lowland malt, and Glen Scotia from Campbeltown) as well as one grain distillery on the site at Alexandria.

Royal Lochnagar

Royal Lochnagar Distillery, Crathie, Ballater, Aberdeenshire

ROYAL LOCHNAGAR Single Highland Malt SCOTCH WHISKY Produced in Scotland BY Royal Lochnagar Distillery

CRATHIE, DEESIDE ABERDEENSHIRE SCOTLAND

70 cl   40 % vol

ESTD 1845

BY APPOINTMENT TO THEIR LATE MAJESTIES QUEEN VICTORIA, KING EDWARD VII & KING GEORGE V

TYPE
Single malt

BOTTLING AGE
12 years, no age given for Selected Reserve

STRENGTH
40%, 43% (Selected Reserve)

TASTE RATING
3–4

MINIATURES
Yes

COMMENTS
A big-bodied, rich and highly fruity malt with a delightfully sherried flavour. Royal Lochnagar Selected Reserve, with a more robust taste, is also available.

VISITORS
Visitors are welcome 1000–1700 Mon.–Fri all year. Telephone 01339-742273.

Lochnagar Distillery was built in 1826 by James Robertson, an infamous local illicit distiller, on the slopes of the mountain from which it took its name. Distilling was not peaceful work at that time: Lochnagar was destroyed by fire, reputedly the work of rival illicit distillers, in 1841 before being taken over and rebuilt by John Begg four years later Its 'Royal' prefix came after a visit and tasting in 1848 by Queen Victoria (who was said to be partial to whisky) and Prince Albert, who were staying at nearby Balmoral. The distillery was bought by Dewar, is now owned by United Distillers and is licensed to John Begg Ltd.

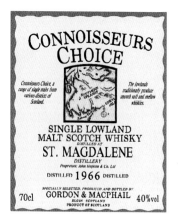

St Magdalene

*St Magdalene Distillery,
Linlithgow, West Lothian*

TYPE
Single malt

BOTTLING AGE
Varies

STRENGTH
Varies

TASTE RATING
2–3

MINIATURES
Yes

COMMENTS
A light-bodied Lowland malt, smooth and generally dry yet with a hint of fruity sweetness. Available only from independent merchants and their retail outlets, its produce can be difficult to find.

St Magdalene, built on the lands of St Mary's Cross towards the end of the nineteenth century, was until recently the sole survivor of the six distilleries which existed in Linlithgow in the last century. Linlithgow had once been a centre of brewing and distilling due to an abundance of barley and fine water from local supplies. All the distillery's production officially went into blends, although it is still available through independent bottlers. St Magdalene was closed by its owners, United Distillers, in the mid 1980s, the building subsequently being converted to private housing.

Scapa

*Scapa Distillery,
Kirkwall, Orkney*

TYPE
Single malt

BOTTLING AGE
Varies

STRENGTH
Varies

TASTE RATING
3

MINIATURES
Yes

COMMENTS
Scapa is available mainly from independent bottlers and is a medium-bodied malt with a dryish, heathery flavour which is complemented by a satisfyingly malty sweetness.

VISITORS
The distillery has no reception centre, but visitors are welcome by appointment. Telephone 01856-872071 to arrange.

PURE MALT SCOTCH WHISKY
from
SCAPA
(ORKNEY)
Distillery
Proprietors: Taylor & Ferguson Ltd.

Bottled by Wm. Cadenhead,
18 Golden Square, Aberdeen
Scotland

75 cl   46% vol

Scapa is one of two distilleries in Kirkwall (Highland Park being the other), yet despite their proximity, their whiskies taste quite different. Scapa was built in 1885 by Macfarlane and Townsend – the latter already a well-known distiller on Speyside – and was bought by Hiram Walker in 1954. It is now owned by Allied Distillers who send most of its produce for blending, but also market the single largely through duty-free outlets. The distillery overlooks the giant natural bay of Scapa Flow, a major Royal Navy anchorage in both world wars. The German fleet was scuttled there during the First World War, and the distillery itself was saved from destruction by fire by ships in the bay around that time.

Scotia Royale

*Gibson Scotch Whisky
Distilleries Ltd,
Glasgow*

TYPE
De luxe

BOTTLING AGE
12 years

STRENGTH
40%, 43%

TASTE RATING
2–3

MINIATURES
Yes

COMMENTS
A medium-bodied de luxe blend, Scotia Royale is a smooth, well-balanced whisky with a hint of peat. Glen Scotia malt is one of this whisky's most important ingredients.

Scotia Royale is one of a range of whiskies, including the popular blend Fraser McDonald and Royal Culross vatted malt, which are associated with the Glen Scotia Distillery in Campbeltown. All three are produced by Gibson Scotch Whisky Distilleries Ltd, a subsidiary of the Loch Lomond Distillery Co. Ltd of Alexandria. The company now has three malt distilleries (Loch Lomond which produces Inchmurrin, a Highland malt, Littlemill, a Lowland malt, and Glen Scotia from Campbeltown) as well as one grain distillery on the site at Alexandria.

The Singleton of Auchroisk

Auchroisk Distillery, Mulben, Banffshire

TYPE
Single malt

BOTTLING AGE
Minimum 10 years

STRENGTH
40%

TASTE RATING
2–3

MINIATURES
Yes

COMMENTS
This whisky is medium-bodied, with a hint of peat to its flavour, which is smooth and sweet, derived from part-maturation in sherry casks.

VISITORS
Visitors are welcome by appointment on weekdays. Telephone 01542-8606333 to arrange.

*O*ne of the newest Scots whisky distilleries (opened in 1974), Auchroisk was built by International Distillers and Vintners and is licensed to Justerini & Brooks. Dorie's Well provides the distillery with its pure, natural water source. The building itself has won several awards, including one from the Angling Foundation for not interfering with the progress of local salmon as they swim upriver. The company has been marketing its single malt since 1987 but it is already a winner of twelve major awards.

Speyburn

*Speyburn-Glenlivet
Distillery,
Rothes, Moray*

TYPE

Single malt

BOTTLING AGE

10 years

STRENGTH

40%

TASTE RATING

3–4

MINIATURES

Yes

COMMENTS

A medium-bodied whisky with a firm yet subtle flavour and a dry, warming, peaty finish.

VISITORS

The distillery is not open to visitors.

Speyburn was built in 1897 on the outskirts of Rothes, and outwardly has hardly been altered in the past century. Set among rolling green slopes, it is one of the most picturesque distilleries in Scotland. It was originally built for the blenders John Hopkins and later acquired by United Distillers. Its produce was difficult to find as a single malt until it was bought from UD in 1992 by the independent Inver House Distillers, also producers of An Cnoc malt, Pinwinnie de luxe blend and Heather Cream liqueur.

Springbank

*Springbank Distillery,
Campbeltown, Argyllshire*

TYPE
Single malt

BOTTLING AGE
12, 15, 21, 25, 30 years

STRENGTH
46%

TASTE RATING
4

MINIATURES
Yes

COMMENTS
Often described as a classic malt, Springbank is a smooth, mellow whisky, light yet complex and full-flavoured.

VISITORS
The distillery is open to visitors strictly by appointment. Telephone 01586-552085 to arrange.

Springbank was built in 1828 by the Mitchell family, previous owners of an illicit still in the area. The distillery is still owned today by the founders' family, and has never been closed at any time in its history. It is presently the only remaining working distillery in Campbeltown, the only Scots town with its own regional whisky classification to reflect the proliferation of distilleries which could be found here in the past. Along with Glenfiddich, Springbank is unusual in bottling on the premises, and is also the only Scottish distillery to carry out the full malt whisky production process, from floor malting to bottling. Springbank is not coloured with caramel, and is the only malt sold under a distillery label which has not been chill filtered. Longrow single malt is also produced here.

Stag's Breath Liqueur

Meikles of Scotland,
Newtonmore, Inverness-shire

TYPE
Liqueur

STRENGTH
19.8%

TASTE RATING
2

MINIATURES
Yes

COMMENTS
A light and smooth union of fine Speyside whisky with heather comb honey. Equally suited to a role as an aperitif or as a digestif.

VISITORS
Meikles have no visitor facilties at present.

Meikles of Scotland is a small Speyside family firm and has been producing Stag's Breath since 1989. The liqueur takes its name from one of the fictional whiskies lost at sea in Sir Compton Mackenzie's famous re-telling of the wartime sinking of the SS *Politician*, in his book, *Whisky Galore*.

Stewarts Cream of the Barley

Allied Distillers,
Dumbarton, Dunbartonshire

TYPE
Blend

STRENGTH
40%

TASTE RATING
2

MINIATURES
Yes

COMMENTS
A popular and good-quality blend with a soft and well-balanced, sweetish, malty flavour.

VISITORS
The plant is not suitable for visitors.

Stewart & Son of Dundee was founded in 1831 and was one of the first companies to exploit newer methods of distilling – particularly the new patent still – and the beginnings of the market for blended whiskies. The company grew steadily in size and the brand in popularity. It was bought by Allied-Lyons in 1969 and today operates under Allied Distillers as one of their most popular standard blends for the UK market.

"STRATHISLA"
PURE HIGHLAND MALT
SCOTCH WHISKY
THE OLDEST DISTILLERY IN THE HIGHLANDS

AGED **12** YEARS

70cl e   DISTILLED AND BOTTLED BY CHIVAS BROTHERS LTD   43%vol
STRATHISLA DISTILLERY, KEITH, AB55 3BS, SCOTLAND

Strathisla

*Strathisla Distillery,
Keith, Banffshire*

TYPE
Single malt

BOTTLING AGE
12 years

STRENGTH
43%

TASTE RATING
4

MINIATURES
Yes

COMMENTS
A big, robust whisky which is full-flavoured and fruity, with a nutty, sherried sweetness.

VISITORS
Visitors are welcome 0930–1600 Mon.–Fri., all year, 0930–1600 Sat., Jul.–Aug. Telephone 01542-783044.

*A*ccording to records, production of a 'heather ale' by local clerics had been taking place in this area as early as 1208. The later siting of Milton Distillery (as Strathisla was formerly known) here in the eighteenth century may have been for the same reasons: set in a good barley-producing area, with easy access to a pure local spring which had been a holy well of local Cistercian monks, and said to be guarded by water spirits. The distillery, one of the oldest and most picturesque in the Highlands, passed through several hands until it was bought by Chivas Brothers, a Seagram subsidiary, in 1950.

Talisker

*Talisker Distillery, Carbost,
Isle of Skye*

TYPE
Single malt

BOTTLING AGE
8, 10 years

STRENGTH
45.8%

TASTE RATING
5

MINIATURES
Yes

COMMENTS
Talisker is Skye's only malt and has been described as being mid-way between Islay and Highland malts. It is full-bodied with a rich, peaty flavour and elements of malty, fruity sweetness.

VISITORS
Visitors are welcome 0930–1630 Mon.–Fri., Apr.–Oct., and by appointment 1400–1630 Nov.–Mar. Telephone 0147-842203.

*T*alisker Distillery had an inauspicious start in the 1830s, being denounced by a local minister as a great curse for the area. Despite his disapproval, distilling has continued successfully, with the distillery changing hands several times. A victim of several fires throughout its 160-year history, it was almost completely rebuilt in 1960. The distillery is owned today by United Distillers, and some of its product goes into Johnnie Walker blends. The single malt appears in UD's Classic Malts series, and was even praised by exile Robert Louis Stevenson in his poem, *The Scotsman's Return from Abroad*, as one of 'The King o' drinks'.

Tamdhu

Tamdhu Distillery,
Knockando, Aberlour,
Banffshire

TYPE
Single malt

BOTTLING AGE
No age given

STRENGTH
40%, 43%

TASTE RATING
3

MINIATURES
Yes

COMMENTS
A good, light-to-medium Speyside malt, which is slightly peaty but with a delicate sweetness and a long, subtle finish.

VISITORS
The distillery is not open to visitors.

*H*ighland Distilleries bought this distillery shortly after it opened in 1897 and have owned it ever since. It was extensively refurbished in the 1970s and is now one of the most modern distilleries on Speyside. Set in the Spey valley, Tamdhu used to favour the hyphenated Glenlivet suffix, but this has been dropped in recent years. As well as its appearance as a single malt, Tamdhu features in The Famous Grouse blend, owned by Highland's subsidiary, Matthew Gloag & Son.

Tamnavulin

Tamnavulin Distillery,
Tomnavoulin, Banffshire

TYPE
Single malt

BOTTLING AGE
10 years

STRENGTH
40%

TASTE RATING
3

MINIATURES
Yes

COMMENTS
A lightish, mellow Glenlivet-type malt with a sweetish bouquet and taste but an underlying grapey note.

Opened in 1966, this was one of the newest Highland distilleries. A rather functional building, it is set on slopes above the River Livet and used water from a nearby burn. This is another distillery which once carried the hyphenated Glenlivet suffix but has since shed it. Tamnavulin was owned until 1993 by Invergordon Distillers, but Whyte & Mackay acquired the group that year. Since then production has been mothballed here and at two of the other former Invergordon malt distilleries, Tullibardine and Bruichladdich.

Teacher's Highland Cream

Allied Distillers,
Dumbarton, Dunbartonshire

TYPE
Blend

STRENGTH
40%, 43%

TASTE RATING

2

MINIATURES
Yes

COMMENTS
Teacher's Highland Cream is a superior blend which has a smooth, sweet flavour with a trace of dryer, heathery notes. It is one of the most popular blended whiskies in the UK. Its sister blend is the 12-year-old Teacher's Royal Highland.

VISITORS
The plant is not suitable for visitors.

*T*he Teacher's company was begun in Glasgow in the 1830s by William Teacher, a young man barely in his twenties. The business started with licensed premises where people could drink whisky, and expanded through the years of the nineteenth century to include blending, bottling and export interests. Highland Cream was first marketed in 1884, although Teacher's did not build its first distillery, at Ardmore, until 1898. The company later concentrated on blending, bottling and exporting, selling off its licensed shops. Today the company is owned by Allied Distillers and the blend sells into 150 countries.

Teaninich

*Teaninich Distillery,
Alness, Ross-shire*

TYPE
Single malt

BOTTLING AGE
10 years

STRENGTH
43%

TASTE RATING
3

MINIATURES
Yes

COMMENTS
A difficult-to-find single malt,
Teaninich is assertive with a
spicy, smoky and satisfying
taste.

VISITORS
Visitors are welcome by
appointment only. Telephone
01349-882461 to arrange.

HIGHLAND
SINGLE MALT
SCOTCH WHISKY

The *Cromarty Firth* is one of the few places in
the British Isles inhabited by *PORPOISE*. They
can be seen quite regularly. *swimming*
close to the shore *less than a mile* from

TEANINICH

distillery. Founded in 1817 in the *Ross-shire*
town of ALNESS, the *distillery* is now one
of the largest in *Scotland.* TEANINICH
is an assertive *single MALT WHISKY*
with a *spicy,* *smoky, satisfying* taste.

AGED **10** YEARS

Distilled & Bottled in SCOTLAND
TEANINICH DISTILLERY,
Alness, Ross-shire, Scotland

43% vol   70cl

*T*eaninich Distillery dates from
the early 1800s and in 1887 it
was recorded as the only distillery
north of Inverness to be 'lighted by
electricity'. The majority of the
present buildings date from the 1970s
and it is now owned by United
Distillers who reopened it in 1990
after it was mothballed for several
years. Most of the production has traditionally gone into blending, but the
single malt has become easier to find
since its official bottling as part of
UD's Distillery (Flora and Fauna)
Malts series.

Tobermory

Tobermory Distillery,
Tobermory, Isle of Mull

TYPE
Single malt

BOTTLING AGE
No age given

STRENGTH
40%

TASTE RATING
3

MINIATURES
Yes

COMMENTS

A nicely balanced, light malt with a delicate, flowery aroma and drier, heathery tones in its flavour. A good pre-dinner dram.

VISITORS

The Visitor Centre and Distillery Shop are open Mon.–Fri., Easter–30 Sept. Tours can be arranged at other times in the year. Telephone 01688-302645..

Set in a wooded site by the sea, Tobermory Distillery has enjoyed mixed fortunes since it was first established in 1823. It has been closed several times during its existence, most recently in the 1980s when it was mothballed. Having reopened in 1990, the distillery is now back in production. The distillery was previously known as Ledaig, changing its name in the 1970s and a single malt-marketed under the old name is also available. Tobermoray remains one of the few family-owned independent distilleries.

Tomatin

*Tomatin Distillery,
Tomatin, Inverness-shire*

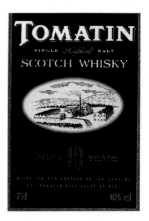

TYPE
Single malt

BOTTLING AGE
10, 12, 25 years

STRENGTH
40%, 43%

TASTE RATING
2

MINIATURES
Yes

COMMENTS
A lightly-peated and delicately flavoured malt which makes a pleasant aperitif.

VISITORS
Visitors are welcome 0900–1630 Mon.–Fri, all year, and 0900–1300 Sat., May–Oct. Large parties must book in advance. Telephone 01808-511444.

*A*t over 1000 feet above sea level, Tomatin is one of Scotland's highest distilleries. Situated in the Monadhliath Mountains from where it draws its water supply, the distillery was established in 1897 (although it is known that whisky has been made on the site since the sixteeth century). A major programme of expansion in the early 1970s made Tomatin the largest distillery in Scotland. Against a background of general decline in the industry, however, the company experienced financial difficulties in the 1980s before being bought by a Japanese consortium, thus becoming the first Scotch whisky distillery to have Japanese owners.

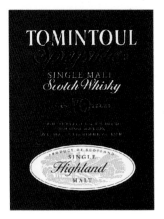

Tomintoul

Tomintoul Distillery,
Ballindalloch, Banffshire

TYPE
Single malt

BOTTLING AGE
10 years

STRENGTH
40%, 43%

TASTE RATING
2–3

MINIATURES
Yes

COMMENTS
A light, delicate whisky with a fine balance of flavours in the Glenlivet style. An ideal dram for beginners, or as an aperitif.

VISITORS
The distillery is not open to visitors.

*B*uilt in 1964 near to Tomintoul, the second-highest village in Scotland and once a centre for illicit distilling, Tomintoul Distillery is also, at 1100 feet, one of the highest in the country. Its water is drawn from the nearby Ballantruan spring. In spite of its scenic location, surrounded by hills and the Glenlivet forest, it is a modern, functional building which lacks the charm associated with the architecture of many older distilleries. Owned until 1993 by Invergordon Distillers, Tomintoul was one of the group's seven malt distilleries which passed into the hands of Whyte & Mackay that year.

The Tormore

*The Tormore Distillery,
Advie, Grantown-on-Spey,
Moray*

TYPE
Single malt

BOTTLING AGE
10 years

STRENGTH
40%, 43%

TASTE RATING
2–3

MINIATURES
Yes

COMMENTS
A medium-bodied whisky, rich and slightly nutty in flavour. An after-dinner dram.

VISITORS
Visitors are welcome by appointment. Telephone 01807-510244.

*B*uilt in 1959, this was Speyside's first new distillery this century. Not a traditional-looking distillery, it is an attractive complex in a pleasant Highland setting, and has the delightfully kitsch touch of a chiming clock which plays the air *Highland Laddie* every hour. Tormore's water comes from the Achvochkie Burn, fed by the nearby Loch an Oir (Lake of Gold). An impressive working model of the Tormore Distillery can be seen at the Scotch Whisky Heritage Centre on Edinburgh's Royal Mile. The distillery itself is owned by Allied Distillers, with some of its produce featuring in their Long John blends.

PRODUCT OF SCOTLAND

Tullibardine

SINGLE HIGHLAND MALT SCOTCH WHISKY

A Single Malt Scotch Whisky of quality and distinction distilled and bottled by
TULLIBARDINE DISTILLERY LIMITED
BLACKFORD   PERTHSHIRE   SCOTLAND

40%vol   70cl

Tullibardine

*Tullibardine Distillery,
Blackford, Perthshire*

TYPE
Single malt

BOTTLING AGE
10 years

STRENGTH
40%

TASTE RATING
2–3

MINIATURES
Yes

COMMENTS
Tullibardine is a good, all-round single malt, full-bodied and with a sweet, well-rounded flavour with a grapey note.

*T*ullibardine Distillery was built on the site of a medieval brewery reputed to have produced ale for the coronation of James IV in 1488. It was opened as a distillery in 1949 and is actually situated at Blackford, a few miles away from Tullibardine village. Tullibardine was one of the seven malt distilleries, previously belonging to Invergordon Distillers, which passed into the ownership of Whyte & Mackay in 1993. Since then production has been mothballed.

Ultima

*Justerini & Brooks,
London*

TYPE

Blend

STRENGTH

43%

TASTE RATING

3

MINIATURES

No

COMMENTS

Ultima is the ultimate blend
and a truly unique creation: a
blend of 116 malts and 12 grain
whiskies, many of which are no
longer being produced. Ultima
has a rich, slightly sweet aroma
with a smooth, dry finish.

*J*usterini & Brooks' principal
founder, Giacomo Justerini, was
a wine merchant from Bologna who
was infatuated by an Italian opera
singer, whom he followed to London
in the mid-eighteenth century. He set
up the wine merchants, Justerini and
Brooks in the capital in 1749 and
began selling Scotch thirty years later.
In 1962 the company built on previous
amalgamations by combining
with W. & A. Gilbey to form International
Distillers and Vintners Ltd
(IDV). Grand Metropolitan bought
IDV, then part of Watney Mann &
Truman, in 1972. The creation of
Ultima represented the fulfilment of a
dream held for many years by J&B's
Master Blender, Jim Milne.

Vat 69

United Distillers,
Kilmarnock, Ayrshire

TYPE
Blend

STRENGTH
43%

TASTE RATING
2

MINIATURES
Yes

COMMENTS

A smooth, well-balanced and distinctly mature blend, light but with a pleasantly malty background.

Sandersons were Leith wine and spirit merchants who moved into whisky blending in the 1860s. William Sanderson was keen to find a notable blend to market and produced 100 different whiskies to be tested, each in numbered casks. The unanimous choice of his associates was the whisky from vat number 69, and so the name suggested itself. It was introduced onto the market in 1882, and William Sanderson's son was responsible for early advertising and marketing successes. Sanderson was also a founder of the North British Distillery company in 1885, ensuring supplies of good grain whisky for his blends. Today Sanderson and its brands are owned by United Distillers.

White Horse

United Distillers,
Glasgow

TYPE

Blend

STRENGTH

43%

TASTE RATING

2–3

MINIATURES

Yes

COMMENTS

White Horse is a smooth and distinctive whisky with peaty elements in both its aroma and flavour. It is the leading standard blend in Japan.

White Horse Distillers, known until 1924 as Mackie & Co., was established by James Logan Mackie in 1861. The company became successful under its second head, Peter Mackie, entrepreneur and the driving force who registered the name 'White Horse', called after a famous Edinburgh coaching inn, for his blend in 1890. By the time he died in 1924 his whisky was one of the foremost blends in the world. Three years later White Horse Distillers joined the Distillers Company Ltd, with whom Mackie had had difficult relations during his lifetime. White Horse also produce Logan and White Horse Extra Fine, de luxe blends for the export market.

Whyte & Mackay Special Reserve

Whyte & Mackay, Glasgow

TYPE
Blend

STRENGTH
43%

TASTE RATING
2

MINIATURES
Yes

COMMENTS

A good quality, smooth, light-bodied whisky with a well-rounded, mellow sweetness. This is said to come from the particular blending process the company uses, vatting the component malts together in sherry butts for at least six months, and then adding the grain content before leaving the resulting blend to mature further.

*J*ames Whyte and Charles Mackay, both whisky merchants, began their partnership and blending firm in 1882. Sales and the company expanded steadily throughout the late nineteenth century and into the twentieth, although their main markets were always overseas. The company merged with Dalmore Distillery, with whom it had had a long-standing relationship, in the 1960s, and acquired two more distilleries, Fettercairn and Tomintoul-Glenlivet, after a merger with Sir Hugh Fraser's Scottish & Universal Investments Ltd. in 1972. In 1993 the Whyte & Mackay Group acquired Invergordon Distillers, adding four more malt distilleries and a grain distillery to their holdings. Whyte & Mackay also produce 12-year-old and 21-year-old blends.

William Grant's Family Reserve

Girvan Distillery,
Girvan, Ayrshire

TYPE
Blend

STRENGTH
43%

TASTE RATING
2

MINIATURES
Yes

COMMENTS
A traditional yet individual blend of smooth character with a light, fresh taste which incorporates elements of Glenfiddich and The Balvenie.

VISITORS
The plant is not open to visitors.

*T*he Grants of Glenfiddich, producers of the world's biggest-selling single malt whisky, are responsible for the production of two blends: William Grant's Family Reserve and Grant's 12 Years Old, the latter being a de luxe blend. The company began as malt whisky distillers in 1887 at Glenfiddich, moving into blending and exporting in 1898 after Pattison, one of the largest blenders and wholesale merchants, and Grant's biggest buyers, went bankrupt. In 1962 the company built a large complex at Girvan, housing a grain distillery, a malt distillery (Ladyburn, now dismantled), and blending facilities. Blended products are bottled at a site in Paisley.

Irish

The History of Whiskey-making in Ireland

*T*he origins of whiskey making in Ireland are just as obscure as in its Scots cousin. The traditional folktales too, which have grown up to guesstimate at its origins are not dissimilar: visitors to Arab lands – this time, sixth-century missionary monks – are credited with having the good sense to return with the secrets of their hosts' distillation processes.

As with the Scots Gaelic, the Irish Gelic term *uisce beatha* is the root of the drink's anglicized name. The story goes that the first to begin the process of anglicization were Ireland's English invaders, the forces of Henry II who first arrived in 1170 AD.

To borrow an Italian saying, if the stories are not true, they are a happy invention, and the real tale will undoubtedly never be known. In any case, by the sixteenth century whiskey production and consumption was widespread. It would not be fanciful to suggest that every area had its own still and the drink was a commonplace of Irish life, whether for its medicinal properties or for simply for the pleasure of drinking it. Consumption spread beyond Ireland, too: Elizabeth I of England was known to be fond of whiskey and one of her more famous courtiers, Sir Walter Raleigh, was the glad recipient of a cask as he set off on his travels. It was well enough travelled even to reach the court of the Russian tsar, Peter the Great.

Taxes on Irish whiskey were introduced in the mid-seventeenth century after the English Civil War by a cash-strapped government in London, and while their enforcement was ineffective enough to be subverted by bribery, stealth or simply by ignoring them, the new laws and duties did serve to disrupt the unofficial industry, with transgressors facing the threat of severe fines and imprisonment. This is not to suggest that all whiskey producers in Ireland instantly chose to go illegal to escape the exciseman: Ireland claims the distinction of having the world's oldest licensed whiskey distillery. At Bushmills in Co. Antrim there had been a tradition of distilling for centuries, and the first licence was granted in 1608. But generally, as over the water in Scotland, the smaller, illicit stills outnumbered their legal counterparts and the industry

The world's oldest licenced distillery, 'Old Bushmills' (Irish Distillers)

continued to grow until, by the end of the eighteenth century, it was thought that there were up to 2000 stills in the country.

As with the Scotch industry, the Excise Act of 1823 proved a turning point. It overhauled and simplified the tax system, encouraged bigger producers to take out licences, and out-lawed stills under 40-gallons' capacity, those being the most likely to be illegal. Some of the bigger producers, most notably the Dublin family concerns such as Jameson and Power, grabbed the opportunity to capitalise on their already high reputations, increase the size of their operations and consoli-date their share of the spirits market. By the late nineteenth century the future of Irish whiskey looked bright: it was among the most popular spirits in the western world, and by the time the Phylloxera blight struck French vineyards in the 1806s, decimating supplies of brandy, there were over 150 Irish distillers producing over 400 brands, who were able to seize an advantage from the situation. But developments were already taking place which would ultimately see Scotch whisky, considered by the Irish to be an inferior product, out-strip it in the marketplace.

The Irish distillers were to prove themselves singularly unable to read new developments in their market in the com-ing decades. The first significant event was the invention by Aeneas Coffey, the former Irish Inspector General of Excise, of a continuous patent still. Patented in 1832, the Coffey, or patent still produced a light grain spirit which could be used in a mix with malt whiskey to mellow its full-bodied flavour for the untutored palate. The Irish producers' disdain for such a new departure was not shared by the makers of Scotch, who seized the chance to adulterate their fiercer spirit into a more widely acceptable blended product. Although generally acknowledged as having a finer flavour, Irish whiskey, with producers content to rest on their laurels, began to be caught and overtaken in the popularity stakes by the new, aggressively marketed Scotch blends.

An unexpected blow came from the political situation in Ireland. Residual bad feeling after the War of Independence and a bruising trade war between Britain and the new Irish Free State denied the whiskey industry access to Britain and its imperial markets from the early 1920s.

An already bad state of affairs was worsened by developments in the United States, one of the biggest markets for Irish. The Prohibition laws on the sale of alcohol, in force from 1920 to 1933, hit the Irish industry hard and, ironically, whiskey's very popularity ultimately served to give it a bad name in the US. When supplies of the legal stuff ran out, American bootleggers didn't hesitate to call their illicitly distilled fire-water by Irish names to capitalise on the real spirit's popularity. Inevitably its reputation suffered, but the real body-blow in the American market was dealt yet again by the Irish producers' inability to anticipate developments: maturing stocks had been allowed to run down during the Prohibition period, with the result that the industry was unable to meet the return to full demand in 1933. The Scotch blended industry suffered fewer such problems, and it swallowed up the market share of Irish in the US.

These errors of judgement and historical accident together depressed the fortunes of Irish whiskey for several decades.

Although the spirit continued to be as popular as ever at home, export markets virtually dried up and the industry atrophied, with some smaller and medium-sized distilleries closing for good. A turnaround finally began in 1966 when the South's largest distilleries joined forces to create the Irish Distillers Group. The addition a few years later of Bushmills from the North ensured a concentration of all-Irish marketing power. One instantly recognisable result of the amalgamation was that all Irish whiskey was henceforth spelled with 'ey' rather than simply 'y'. Previously a practice followed only by the Dublin producers, it now gave Irish an extra, visual distinction from Scotch.

The unfortunate attempts by rival groups at take overs in the Scotch industry were mirrored in the late 1980s in Ireland, with the French Pernod Ricard group ultimately emerging victorious in their attempts to buy Irish Distillers. Irish Distillers' successes, particularly with Bushmills and Jamesons, have been built on by the new owners, raising the profile of Irish whiskey once more beyond its native shores. Whiskey and whiskey lovers everywhere will look for these trends to continue.

The Making of Irish Whiskey

*T*he basic processes and ingredients used in the making of Irish and Scotch whiskies are not dissimilar. Both, of course, observe the traditional steps: malting, mashing, fermentation, distillation and maturation, but it is from the small differences in approach at crucial points that the variations in the taste and character of two spirits lie.

Pot Still Whiskey

(1) **Malting** At the outset, the Irish process varies noticeably from the Scotch. Although barley is the main ingredient of both, the Irish treatment is quite different. The sprouted bar-

Barley being sent to the Jameson Bow St. Distillery, c. 1920 (Irish Distillers)

ley in Irish whiskey is dried in the closed kiln, not over a peat fire – perhaps surprisingly, as Ireland has such an abundance of the fuel. This is then mixed with unmalted barley before being ground into grist. A nineteenth-century tax on malt first encouraged the use of unmalted barley, a necessity-driven innovation which happily proved its worth over the years. The absence of peat-smokiness mixed with the unmalted barley already promise a spirit with a distinct flavour and character.

(2) **Mashing** The processes involved in grinding the grain into grist and then mixing it with water in the mash tun to produce wort are the same in both Irish and Scotch production.

(3) **Fermentation** Once again, the same basic steps are followed in the two procedures: with the wort in the washback, yeast is added to convert the liquid's sugars into alcohol.

(4) **Distillation** The essential principles and processes of distillation are unchanging, whatever the drink being produced, or level of skill of the distiller, or still being

Copper pot stills used in the triple distillation of Irish whiskey (Irish Distillers)

used. The alcohol, with its lower boiling point than water, is steamed off. As with Scotch, the shape of the still also has a part to play in the whiskey's final character, and the Irish stills are generally larger than the Scottish ones. This distilling would generally happen twice in Scotland. But at this stage also, Irish whiskey is usually (although not always) given the further refinement of a third pass through the still. With even more of the lower alcohols left behind, a subtly different-tasting, purer and lighter alcohol is emerging.

(5) **Maturation** The final stage in the production process is the same as for any spirit: the whiskey is transferred into casks to mature for the required number of years – three at legal minimum but more likely to be eight, ten or even longer for some of the top brands. The casks have usually had other occupants – normally sherry, bourbon or rum – although new

Whiskey ageing in oak barrels in the Old Bushmills warehouse (Irish Distillers)

oak casks are also used. Each wood imparts its own flavour, and the final resulting blend in a bottle can be a mix of hundreds of casks.

Grain Whiskey

The processes followed in Ireland for the manufacture of grain whiskey are basically the same as in Scotland. Again, different cereals can be used – wheat, maize and a large proportion of unmalted barley, with distillation taking place in two patent stills. The resulting grain spirit is predominately used in Irish blends. At Midleton Distillery in Co. Cork, the patent stills are also used in conjunction with the pot stills, with the result that some of their whiskey has been distilled five times.

Blending

Although the whiskies in Scotch blends can be 'married' in casks for a year or more to allow infusion of the flavours, in Ireland they are vatted together for a matter of days at most. According to the accepted wisdom in Ireland, this reflects the relative importance of blending in Scotch whisky, where the skills of the blender are crucial to the final product. In Ireland, the theory goes, it is the distiller's art rather than that of the blender's which has by far the greater influence on the whiskey's final taste.

Their disdain for blended, or vatted, whiskies was one of the reasons why Irish distillers lost out in the battle with Scotch for the hearts and favours of the world's whiskey-drinkers. The Irish refused even to recognise the adulterated Scots product as proper whiskey until after it was decreed legitimate by a Royal Commission reporting in 1909. Even until relatively recently, Irish whiskey was sold as pot-still whiskey with no other variation. Now, however, the market is dominated by quality blended whiskies, in response to modern preferences for lighter spirits, and the practice of using mixers with drinks.

Visiting Irish Distilleries

Although Ireland has a limited number of whiskey-industry centres, most cater well for visitors and tourists. The Irish Whiskey Tourist Trail takes in the two ICD distilleries, north and south, as well as offering a glimpse into the whiskey industry's glorious past.

At Bushmills in Co. Antrim, close to the Giant's Causeway, is Old Bushmills Distillery, offering a guided tour of the distillery and a chance to sample and buy its produce. The distillery is open to visitors 0900–1200, 1330–1530 Mon.–Thu., 0900–1145 Fri.; telephone: 01265–731521. There is an entry fee. In Dublin is The Irish Whiskey Corner, housed in warehouses of the old Jameson distillery at Bow Street. Included is an Irish whiskey museum, a bar with tasting session and an opportunity to buy some of your favourites. Tours here are 1530 Mon.–Fri., Nov.–Apr., with an extra tour at 1100, May–Oct. Group tours can be booked in advance; telephone 01 872-5566. There is an entry fee.

Finally, in Midleton is The Jameson Heritage Centre, in and around the old Midleton Distillery buildings, with plenty of fittings still *in situ* in the well-explained walk-around site. A bar and shop round off the facilities. The centre is open 1000–1800 daily, Mar.–Oct. Telephone to check definite opening dates at the beginning and end of the season; telephone 021 613594. There is an entry fee and special rates for groups.

Not on the ICD trail, but well worth a visit for anyone interested in the whiskey industry, social history or industrial archaeology, is Locke's Distillery Museum at Kilbeggan, Co. Westmeath. The distillery was established in 1757, and its machinery dates from Victorian times. It has been restored and opened by the local community – a task which is ongoing – and is a too-unsung highlight of any trip to the Midlands. The centre is open 0900–1800 daily, May–Oct., 1000–1600 daily, Nov.–Mar. Groups are asked to telephone in advance; telephone: 0506-32134.

Poteen

*A*n illicit spirit almost as well-known as its legal equivalent, poteen is so famous that there can hardly be a drinker who has not heard of it. Poteen (or, in Irish, *poitín*, pronounced 'pocheen', with the 'o' sound as in 'pot') has been produced for as long as Irish whiskey has been subject to taxes and laws, and its fame and democratic, accessible nature have secured its place in Irish popular culture. Poteen itself cannot be called whiskey, not least because a much wider variety of ingredients than simply barley can be used (and generally are) and, of course, it is never left for the three years deemed necessary in law to produce a properly matured whiskey!

An illicit poteen still, as depicted in the 1840s

Illicit distillation in most countries was in the past the subject of bitter battles between the distillers and the authorities, and Irish poteen production was no different. An often desperate economic situation for ordinary Irish countrydwellers combined with a British government always vigorous in its dealings with Irish transgressions, to produce several bloody encounters. In the middle were the excisemen: those unlucky enough to be caught by desperate locals might be fortunate to escape with their lives. Anaeas Coffey was seized by such a band and, but for the timely intervention of some troops, would not have lived long enough to invent his patent still.

Generally a colourless liquid, poteen is fiery-tasting and, by nature, less thoroughly distilled than commercially produced whiskies. This lack of precise distillation techniques can be a danger in itself: Brendan Behan related the story of how, during one of his spells in prison, he and his fellow inmates had made their own 'potheen', and a debate had arisen as to the merits of giving the first three drops to the fairies. The more superstitious among them had won out which, as he later discovered, was just as well: 'the first three drops contain a lot of fusel oil which is likely to blind you if you drink it'. Unfortunately even today drinkers are known to have been killed by drinking the foreshots, or by an over-indulgence in poteen itself.

If this has only whetted your appetite to try poteen for yourself but you lack a first-hand supply, commercial versions have been produced. But surely best, and much more interesting and fun, is to find a real-life producer, sit back, and enjoy. You will, after all, be experiencing a piece of authentic Irish.

The
Whiskies
of
Ireland

Taste Rating

The discussions on the different whiskies which follow contain a taste rating of 1–5. This is not intended to be a judgement on the quality or relative standard of the spirit, nor is it possible to place strength and flavour together satisfactorily. Rather, it can be used as an indicator of accessibility of the whisky for a relatively inexperienced palate. A whisky may be mild or strong and still either lack flavour or exude it, so this rating concerns the degree of flavour, while at the same time allowing for the strength interfering with a person's ability to appreciate the flavour. The basic categories are as follows:

1   Popular with particular palates; spirituous, with a very mild flavour

2   Good for beginners; appealing taste and flavour for most palates at certain times

2–3   Also good for beginners, but a little stronger than **2**. One to return to again and again

3   A dram for everyone; not too powerful, with pleasant sensations

3–4   This should also appeal to most tastes, but is slightly stronger, so the palate requires a little more experience

4   Very pleasing; a stronger spirit, ideal for those with more experience

5   Robust; only for the well developed palate

Baileys

R. & A. Bailey & Co.,
Dublin

TYPE
Cream liqueur

STRENGTH
17%

TASTE RATING
2

MINIATURES
Yes

COMMENTS
Baileys' raisiny-sweet chocolate richness is given added depth by its lingering, whiskey finish.

VISITORS
The plant is not open to visitors.

*F*irst of the Irish cream liqueurs on the market, Baileys has never surrendered its position as pack leader. Launched in 1974, it has been for several years the world's leading liqueur brand and is a product so phenomenally successful that it currently accounts for 1% of Ireland's total export trade. The company is a Gilbey's subsidiary, its name chosen as classically Irish, its product an ingenious coupling of two famous Irish products, cream and whiskey. The whiskey is supplied by Irish Distillers, the cream comes from Co. Cavan and both are blended and bottled in Dublin. The company also produces a lower-calorie and lower-fat Baileys Light, aimed mainly at the US market.

Bow Street

*Bow Street Distillery,
Dublin*

TYPE
Single-distillery Irish whiskey

BOTTLING AGE
Varies

STRENGTH
Varies

TASTE RATING
3

MINIATURES
Yes

COMMENTS
A smooth, sweet Irish whiskey with fragrant and fruity notes. An ideal after-dinner drink.

VISITORS
Visitors are welcome to The Irish Whiskey Corner in part of the old distillery buildings. Tours 1100 & 1530 Mon.–Fri., May–Oct.; 1530 Mon.–Fri., Nov.–Apr. Telephone 01 872-5566.

*E*stablished as a distillery before John Jameson bought it over around 1780, Bow Street had originally been owned by the Steins, another famous family of distillers. But it was under its new owners that the distillery became renowned. As sales of whiskey grew throughout the nineteenth century, the industry's good health was mirrored in the buoyancy of Jameson & Son. At one time the company had over a million gallons of whiskey maturing in Bow Street's cellars which wove rabbit-warren-like under the streets north of the Liffey. But by the mid-twentieth century the old site was too cramped, and the decision was taken after Jameson's merger with the Irish Distillers Group to move distilling to Midleton. Part of the site can still be visited in The Irish Whiskey Corner visitor centre.

Bushmills

*Old Bushmills Distillery,
Bushmills, Co. Antrim*

TYPE
Blend

STRENGTH
40%

TASTE RATING
2

MINIATURES
Yes

COMMENTS
A fresh-bodied whiskey with a light, pleasant flavour and a hint of malty sweetness in the finish. This is the standard blend of the distillery.

VISITORS
Visitors are welcome 0900–1200, 1330–1530 Mon.–Thu., 0900–1145 Fri. Telephone 01265-731521.

Old Bushmills glories in the status of the oldest licensed distillery in the world. It is thought that distilling may have begun on the site as early as the thirteenth century, but the first permit was granted by James VI and I to Sir Thomas Phillipps, a local landowner, in 1608. The site was especially suited for its purpose, standing on the banks of St Columb's Rill, or stream, which flowed over the nearby peaty ground and into the River Bush, and which still provides the distillery with its fresh water supplies today. Belying its antiquity, Old Bushmills is distinctly Victorian-Speyside in appearance – a legacy of its rebuilding and the addition of its pagoda towers after a devastating fire in 1885. Although no longer in use, the towers remain the distinctive landmark of a distinguished distillery.

Bushmills
1608

*Old Bushmills Distillery,
Bushmills, Co. Antrim*

TYPE
De luxe blend

BOTTLING AGE
12 years

STRENGTH
43%

TASTE RATING
2–3

MINIATURES
No

COMMENTS
This relatively new whiskey is subtle and sophisticated in character with rich, malty-sweet notes. The '1608' on the label recalls the date of the first licence to distil at Bushmills.

VISITORS
Visitors are welcome 0900–1200, 1330–1530 Mon.–Thu., 0900–1145 Fri. Telephone 01265-731521.

$\mathcal{N}$ow owned by the Pernod Ricard group, Old Bushmills Distillery has been through several turns of fortune and sets of owners since its founding as a company in 1783. Its initially mixed fortunes were the result of strong local competition from several distillers, many of them illegal! The distillery was closed and re-opened several times and by the turn of the century the company was no stranger to the receivers despite its by-then award-winning whiskies. Its fortunes revived under the ownership of the Boyd family, but after the Second World War it moved inevitably from being a family concern through a succession of larger, corporate buyers until in 1972 it finally joined with the Irish Distillers Group. IDG themselves were bought by Pernod Ricard at the end of the 1980s.

Black Bush

*Old Bushmills Distillery,
Bushmills, Co. Antrim*

TYPE
Blend

STRENGTH
40%

TASTE RATING
2–3

MINIATURES
Yes

COMMENTS
Bushmills' premier blend, Black Bush is a smooth, complex whiskey whose malty nose and mellow, nutty flavours are rounded off with a mellow, sherry-sweet finish.

VISITORS
Visitors are welcome 0900–1200, 1330–1530 Mon.–Thu., 0900–1145 Fri. Telephone 01265-731521.

O f the many 'characters' to have had a hand in Irish distilling, Samuel Boyd, owner of Old Bushmills Distillery in the 1920s, is among the most intriguing. He fitted perfectly the stereotype of the aloof, self-made Scotch-Irishman. His pro-temperance sympathies – he was even thought to write campagning leaflets in his spare time, and never allowed drink in his house – sat oddly alongside a career in the spirits trade in which he rose by his efforts to owning his own wholesale company as well as Bushmills. The distillery benefitted from his middle-class, strict, Victorian approach: although working conditions were never luxurious, his unflamboyant, steady-as-she-goes style was able to set the company on a sound footing, in the process beginning a family connection lasting three generations.

Bushmills 5 Years Old *Malt*

Old Bushmills Distillery, Bushmills, Co. Antrim

TYPE
Single malt

BOTTLING AGE
5 years

STRENGTH
40%

TASTE RATING
2

MINIATURES
Yes

COMMENTS
A smooth, nicely balanced Irish malt which is both light and sweet, this is ideal as an aperitif.

VISITORS
Visitors are welcome 0900–1200, 1330–1530 Mon.–Thu., 0900–1145 Fri. Telephone 01265-731521.

*A*lthough it was only one of many distilleries in an area which was also famous for its abundant poteen production, Bushmills has emerged as the region's only survivor. Despite a few close calls, the company has been able to rely at crucial moments on some sound commercial judgement and plain old good luck to see it through the difficult times – as, for example, in the ending of Prohibition in the US, when buoyant stock levels allowed Bushmills to reap the rewards after the difficulties had ended. Its increasingly strong trading position saw it benefit from industry rationalization in the second half of the twentieth century, as in its gradual swallowing-up of the operations of Coleraine Distillery, and it has emerged from its amalgamations with the promise of a secure future.

Bushmills
10 Years Old Malt

Old Bushmills Distillery,
Bushmills, Co. Antrim

TYPE
Single malt

BOTTLING AGE
10 years

STRENGTH
40%

TASTE RATING
2–3

MINIATURES
Yes

COMMENTS
Light and delicately sweet, Bushmills Malt has a rich, malty flavour and a pleasingly dry finish.

VISITORS
Visitors are welcome 0900–1200, 1330–1530 Mon.–Thu., 0900–1145 Fri. Telephone 01265-731521.

Old Bushmills Distillery has enjoyed some sound management and a share of luck throughout its history. But at the backbone of its survival and successes has been the quality of the spirit it has produced, with a portfolio of distinguished whiskies across the production spectrum. In 1897 the distillery marked Queen Victoria's diamond jubilee by its first production of pure malt, specially produced whiskey which retailed at fifty shillings a case! (For many years in the past century Bushmills proudly proclaimed its status as Ireland's only producer of single malt.) A far bigger event is set to be marked with the bottling of Bushmills Millenium, a twenty-five-years-old whiskey for the new century. Bushmills' prospects for success look set to continue.

Carolans

*T. J. Carolan & Son Ltd,
Clonmel, Co. Tipperary*

TYPE

Cream liqueur

STRENGTH

17%

TASTE RATING

2

MINIATURES

Yes

COMMENTS

A pleasantly smooth, honeyed, toffee-sweet Irish whiskey and spirit liqueur.

VISITORS

The plant is not open to visitors.

*F*irst launched in 1978, Carolans is another Irish success story and second only to Baileys in the world Irish cream liqueur market. T. J. Carolan & Son is now owned by C&C International, the Dublin-based wines and spirits group who own, among others, Tullamore Dew whiskey and Irish Mist liqueur. The company also produces Carolans Light, lower in fat and alcoholic content (at 15% abv) than the original, and Carolans Irish Coffee Cream, a newer brand produced especially for the North American market.

Finest Quality

COLERAINE

iRish whiskey

DISTILLED
BLENDED AND BOTTLED BY
THE OLD BUSHMILLS DISTILLERY CO LTD
BUSHMILLS Co. ANTRIM

40% vol   produce of Ireland   700 ml e

Coleraine

*Old Bushmills Distillery,
Bushmills, Co. Antrim*

TYPE
Blend

STRENGTH
40%

TASTE RATING
2

MINIATURES
No

COMMENTS
A fresh, light, sweet blend with a pleasantly rounded character.

VISITORS
Coleraine Distillery is no longer operational, but visitors are welcome at Old Bushmills, where Coleraine whiskey is produced, 0900–1200, 1330–1530 Mon.–Thu., 0900–1145 Fri. Telephone 01265-731521.

*P*reviously one of the most respected of Ireland's distilleries, Coleraine fell victim to the decline and rationalisation of the Irish whiskey industry this century. Distilling had been going on in the Coleraine area since the early seventeenth century, although the distillery itself did not become operational until over two hundred years later. Its reputation was high in the later nineteenth century, to the extent that Coleraine supplied whiskey to the House of Commons, subsequently selling their product under the name of 'Old Irish HC'. But like so many Irish distilleries, Coleraine suffered badly in the twentieth century, eventually being bought by the owners of Bushmills. Production continued very intermittently, latterly in grain whiskey, until closure came in 1978.

Connemara

Cooley Distillery,
Dundalk, Co. Louth

TYPE
Single malt

STRENGTH
40%

TASTE RATING
2–3

MINIATURES
No

COMMENTS
A drier single malt than Tyrconnell, its sister from the Cooley stable, this is a smooth, medium-bodied whiskey. Its soft and unassertive peaty flavour betrays its unique position as Ireland's only peated single malt.

VISITORS
Cooley Distillery is not open to visitors. However, visitors are welcome to Locke's Distillery Museum at Kilbeggan 0900–1800 daily, Apr.–Oct., 1000–1600 Nov.–Mar. Groups please telephone in advance; tel: 0506-32134.

PURE POT STILL
Connemara

PEATED SINGLE MALT
40% vol. **IRISH WHISKEY** 75 cl ℮

Distilled, Matured & Bottled in Ireland. Cooley Distillery Plc, Riverstown, Dundalk, Co. Louth.

• PRODUCT OF IRELAND •

aunched in 1996, Connemara is one of the newest brands from the forward-looking young Cooley Distillery, which began production in 1989. Formerly Ceimici Teo Distillery, it was bought in 1987 by entrepreneur John Teeling who had been keen for several years to enter the whiskey market. The takeover by Pernod Ricard of the Irish Distillers Group in the same year meant that by the time the Cooley Distillery whiskies came of age in 1992 after their required three-year maturation period, they offered the sole alternative to the Pernod/IDG monopoly. The Cooley whiskies are shipped by road to mature in oak-cask-filled warehouses at the old Locke's Distillery buildings in Kilbeggan, Co. Westmeath.

Crested Ten

Midleton Distillery,
Midleton, Co. Cork

TYPE
Blend

STRENGTH
40%

TASTE RATING
2

MINIATURES
No

COMMENTS
A smooth, easy-to-drink Irish blend with an unassertive dryness to complement its sweeter, malty notes.

VISITORS
Visitors are welcome to The Jameson Heritage Centre at Midleton 1000–1800, Mar.–Oct. Telephone 021-613594.

A Jameson whiskey, Crested Ten is produced at the huge Midleton Distillery in Co. Cork where the Dublin company moved from their premises in the capital in 1975. By then, their old distillery at Bow Street – which once held over a million gallons of whiskey maturing in its honeycomb of cellars below the streets – had become too cramped. Today, over a dozen different whiskies, each with its own unique and individual character, are produced side-by-side in the remarkable Midleton Distillery. Visitors who wish to see how it used to be done can also visit part of the Bow Street site in The Irish Whiskey Corner visitor centre.

The Dubliner

The Dubliner Liqueur &
Spirit Co., Dublin

TYPE

Cream liqueur

STRENGTH

17%

TASTE RATING

2

MINIATURES

No

COMMENTS

A relatively late addition to the
Irish cream liqueur market, The
Dubliner is a smooth, mellow
chocolate-cream liqueur.

VISITORS

The plant is not open to
visitors

The Dubliner is the newest
arrival to the Baileys family of
Irish cream liqueurs, the biggest-selling cream liqueurs group in the
world. It is produced, together with
Emmets and O'Darby, in the company's plant at Bailieboro, Co. Cavan.

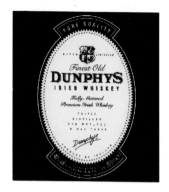

Dunphy's

*Midleton Distillery,
Midleton, Co. Cork*

TYPE
Blend

STRENGTH
40%

TASTE RATING
1

MINIATURES
No

COMMENTS
Blended especially for the export market and for mixing, this is a lighter-bodied Irish with a crisp, fresh palate and slightly spiritous finish.

VISITORS
Visitors are welcome to The Jameson Heritage Centre at Midleton. 1000–1800, Mar.–Oct. Telephone 021-613594.

*P*roduced for the first time in the 1950s, Dunphy's blend was dreamed up by a marketing department at Cork Distilleries Co. quick to capitalise on the contemporary fashion, notably in the US, for Irish coffee (with whiskey). The result was a blend meant to complement its co-ingredients, and not to taste too overpowering. Dunphy's has since been withdrawn from the US market, but is still produced at Midleton Distillery, primarily for home consumption.

Eblana

Cooley Distillery,
Dundalk, Co. Louth

TYPE
Liqueur

STRENGTH
40%

TASTE RATING
2

MINIATURES
No

COMMENTS
A newcomer to the Irish drinks scene, Eblana is an after-dinner liqueur with a rich texture and creamy, nutty-sweet flavours.

VISITORS
Cooley Distillery is not open to visitors. However, visitors are welcome to Locke's Distillery Museum at Kilbeggan 0900–1800 daily, Apr.–Oct., 1000–1600 Nov.–Mar. Groups please telephone in advance; tel: 0506-32134.

*A*dam Millar & Co. was an old name in Dublin distilling, first established in 1843 and based near the Guinness brewery on the Liffey's south bank, and their whiskey was popular in Ireland, and particularly in Dublin, from the earlier part of the twentieth century right up to the 1970s. Adam Millar was bought over by the Cooley Distillery who have now relaunched Millars Special Reserve whiskey. Although on the market only since 1994, it is already an award winner. Eblana, a whiskey liqueur, has also now been launched under the Millar label, Eblana being an ancient Irish name for Dublin.

Emmets

*R. & J. Emmet & Co.,
Dublin*

TYPE
Cream liqueur

STRENGTH
17%

TASTE RATING
2

MINIATURES
No

COMMENTS
Emmets is a creamy, sweet and gently whiskied liqueur with chocolate and toffee flavours and a gentle, mellow finish.

VISITORS
The plant is not open to visitors.

*A*nother liqueur offering from the Gilbey's stable who produce several of the foremost Irish cream liqueurs, including Sheridans and Dubliner, and whose R. & A. Bailey subsidiary manufacture the eponymous top-selling liqueur. Emmets had previously been a stablemate of O'Darby, another cream liqueur, and Gilbey's parent company, International Distillers and Vintners Ltd (IDV) acquired both in 1991, confirming their dominant position in the cream liqueurs market. Emmets is named after Irish patriot and United Irishman Robert Emmet who was executed in 1803 after leading an unsuccessful revolt against British rule.

Green Spot

Mitchell & Son, Dublin

TYPE

Pot still

STRENGTH

40%

TASTE RATING

3

MINIATURES

No

COMMENTS

A traditional and, apart from at Mitchell's premises in Kildare St, hard-to-find whiskey. It is rich and complex and characterized by bags of typical pot-still character.

*D*istilled by John Jameson & Son, Green Spot pot-still whiskey has been produced by Dublin wine and spirit merchants Mitchell & Son for over eighty years. It is the only brand still produced specifically for an independent wine merchant in Ireland to sell under its own name, and the only one remaining from a range of 'coloured spot' whiskies formerly marketed by Mitchell's, a family-run firm which has been in business since 1805. The Kildare Street firm is now unique in Dublin, being the capital's last remaining wine merchant's shop.

Hewitts

*Midleton Distillery,
Midleton, Co. Cork*

TYPE
Blend

STRENGTH
40%

TASTE RATING
2–3

MINIATURES
No

COMMENTS
This is a rich blend whose nutty and malty flavours are overlain by a lighter, fragrant sweetness. It is a difficult-to-find brand.

VISITORS
Visitors are welcome to The Jameson Heritage Centre at Midleton 1000–1800, Mar.–Oct. Telephone 021-613594

*H*ewitts whiskey commemorates the name of a founder of a family-owned Cork distillery which began production in the late eighteenth century. The company was one of the five south-western distilleries who joined together to form the Cork Distillers Co. in 1866 in an effort to take on the might and commercial dominance of the Dublin whiskey companies, most notably Jameson and Power. When the Irish Distilleries Group was formed in 1966, the former rivals came together under the one flag, and the distillery stopped making its grain whiskey in 1975. Hewitts is one of the smaller brands produced by the IDG complex at Midleton.

Inishowen

*Cooley Distillery,
Dundalk, Co. Louth*

TYPE
Blend

STRENGTH
40%

TASTE RATING
2

MINIATURES
No

COMMENTS
The newly revived Inishowen is a smooth, easy-to-drink blend with a refreshing gentle peatiness.

VISITORS
Cooley Distillery is not open to visitors. However, visitors are welcome to Locke's Distillery Museum at Kilbeggan 0900–1800 daily, Apr.–Oct., 1000–1600 Nov.–Mar. Groups please telephone in advance; tel: 0506-32134.

With the launch in 1996 of Inishowen, the independent Cooley Distillery has continued its practice of reviving old and respected names from the past of the Irish whiskey industry. Like Tyrconnell, Inishowen was originally a brand of the Londonderry distillery of A. A. Watt & Co., who traced their commercial origins back to the mid eighteenth century. But Watt's was one of the companies hard hit by US Prohibition in the 1920s, giving the Scottish DCL conglomerate the opportunity to buy out then close down a rival distillery. The company continued to trade only as a blenders until 1970, but its remaining assets were later merged with the new Cooley Distillery company.

Irish Mist

*Irish Mist Liqueur Co.,
Tullamore, Co. Offaly*

TYPE
Liqueur

STRENGTH
35%

TASTE RATING
2

MINIATURES
Yes

COMMENTS
A smooth and mellow blend of whiskies, fragrant herbs and an exotic heather honey.

VISITORS
The plant is not open to visitors.

*O*ne of the longest-lasting and most successful liqueurs on the market, Irish Mist is owned by Dublin-based C&C International, whose other brands include Tullamore Dew whiskey and Carolans cream liqueur. It drew on the centuries-old notion of an Irish heather wine drunk in medieval times and was produced at Tullamore Distillery to make its first appearance on the market in the early 1950s. The distillery, in common with others in Ireland, was in financial difficulties at the time, and whiskey production was just coming to an end, never to resume. Ownership of Tullamore and its products passed first to Irish Distillers then, in 1993, to C&C International.

Jameson

Midleton Distillery, Midleton, Co. Cork

TYPE
Blend

STRENGTH
40%

TASTE RATING
2

MINIATURES
Yes

COMMENTS
Jameson's has a mellow sweetness balanced by fresher, floraly notes. Regarded by many as the classic of its type, this is the biggest selling Irish whiskey outside Ireland.

VISITORS
Visitors are welcome to The Jameson Heritage Centre at Midleton 1000–1800, Mar.–Oct. Telephone 021-613594.

*T*he arrival in Ireland of Scot John Jameson in the 1770s marked a significant new departure for the growing legal Irish whiskey industry. Jameson already had connections with the Scottish industry – he had even married into the Haig family – and his son consolidated the business by marrying a daughter of John Stein, whose family who were among the biggest grain distillers in Scotland and who owned Dublin's Bow Street distillery which Jameson Senior was soon to purchase. His exacting standards and aptitude for the business helped build his firm in the eighteenth century and into the nineteenth. Although own-label sales were still a concept of the future, Jameson's whiskey, sold through merchants, acquired the reputation, with Power's, of being the best of Irish.

AGED **12** YEARS

JAMESON

DISTILLERY RESERVE

IRISH WHISKEY

Matured in
Oak Casks for not less than
twelve years

40%vol. PRODUCT OF IRELAND 700ml℮

Jameson Distillery Reserve

Midleton Distillery, Midleton, Co. Cork

TYPE
Blend

BOTTLING AGE
12 years

STRENGTH
40%

TASTE RATING
3

MINIATURES
No

COMMENTS
A rich, smooth and sherried whiskey with some complementary dry notes in its finish. Distillery Reserve can only be bought at Midleton Distillery.

VISITORS
Visitors are welcome to The Jameson Heritage Centre at Midleton 1000–1800, Mar.–Oct. Telephone 021-613594.

*J*ameson's successes in the nineteenth century were threatened, along with the fortunes of Irish whiskey in general, by an inability to recognise both the threat and the commercial possibilities offered by blending their pure whiskies with grain, a practice which was being adopted enthusiastically and successfully in Scotland. Yet more ground was lost during and after the Prohibition era in the US to the extent that, until surprisingly recently, Jameson's was a product known by few outside Ireland. Happily, that situation was remedied in part by the formation of the Irish Distillers Group, in which the firm was a key player. IDG's takeover by Pernod Ricard has further boosted Jameson's market presence, a trend which the company's other whiskies will hopefully be following.

Jameson *1780*

Midleton Distillery, Midleton, Co. Cork

TYPE
De luxe

BOTTLING AGE
12 years

STRENGTH
40%

TASTE RATING
3

MINIATURES
No

COMMENTS
An elegant whiskey of superior character and a soothingly mellow, sherried flavour. In taste and qualities, not unlike the Distillery Reserve. The label's '1780' refers to the year of Jameson's foundation.

VISITORS
Visitors are welcome to The Jameson Heritage Centre at Midleton 1000–1800, Mar.–Oct. Telephone 021-613594.

*B*y the time the Irish Distillers Group was formed by Jameson's, Power's and the Cork Distilleries Co. in 1966, the Dublin whisky companies were already outgrowing their cramped city-centre premises. The decision to concentrate production at Midleton in Co. Cork saw all the partners eventually move to a new, purpose-built plant there. Today, over a dozen different whiskies, each with their own unique and individual character, are produced side-by-side at this remarkable distillery. Jameson's, the world's favourite Irish whiskey, is one of the star performers in the Midleton line-up.

Established 1842

CADENHEAD'S
AUTHENTIC
COLLECTION

150th anniversary commemoration

Irish Whiskey

This whiskey has been bottled from a selected individual cask in its natural state and shows the character of that cask. It has not been filtered with water, it has not been treated to change its colour and is free from all additives. It has not been subjected to cold filtration but might retain natural constituents and spirit in essence. It is the authentic product of its Distillery.

Bottled by Wm. Cadenhead, 32 Union Street, Campbeltown SCOTLAND

From
POWER's
No.
JOHN'S LANE DISTILLERY
Distilled in 1956 and bottled in 1991
Matured in an oak cask
750ml   for 34 years. 73.2%alc/vol

John's Lane

John's Lane Distillery, Dublin

TYPE
Single-distillery Irish whiskey

BOTTLING AGE
Varies

STRENGTH
Varies

TASTE RATING
3

MINIATURES
Yes

COMMENTS
A medium-bodied whiskey with drier accents offsetting its more fragrant, sweeter flavours.

*J*ohn's Lane Distillery was owned by the Power family, one of Dublin's two big distilling empires. The company was founded in 1791 by James Power, a local inn-keeper who, with his son, built the business rapidly, moving into their new distillery at John's Lane at the start of the new century. Their success was such that, from an initial output of a few thousand gallons a year, production grew to over 300,000 gallons by the 1830s. Not surprisingly the distillery itself was also rebuilt, eventually occupying a seven-acre site by the south side of the Liffey. But harsher times in the twentieth century brought contraction and, ultimately, merger into the Irish Distillers Group in 1966. The John's Lane site was abandoned, and production moved to the IDG plant at Midleton in the 1970s.

Jones Road

Jones Road Distillery,
Dublin

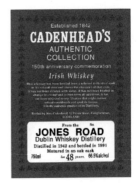

TYPE
Single-distillery Irish whiskey

BOTTLING AGE
Varies

STRENGTH
Varies

TASTE RATING
4

MINIATURES
Yes

COMMENTS
This is a robust, full-bodied whiskey with floral-spicy notes in its sweet flavour, counterbalanced by a powerful dryness.

ones Road Distillery, one of the few non-family whiskey companies in the capital, was established in the 1870s by a group of Dublin entrepreneurs who together formed the Dublin Whiskey Distillery Co. But a glut in the Dublin market meant that by 1889 the company had to merge with two of its city rivals, George Rowe and William Jameson, to form the Dublin Distilling Co. Although resources were pooled, each company produced its own whiskey for a time, but inauspicious trading conditions for Irish whiskey meant that operations were gradually run down in the three distilleries. Jones Road was finally closed in the 1940s.

Kilbeggan

*Cooley Distillery,
Dundalk, Co. Louth*

TYPE
Blend

STRENGTH
40%

TASTE RATING
2

MINIATURES
Yes

COMMENTS
Pleasant, clean and slightly sweet, this is a smooth blend with across-the-board appeal.

VISITORS
Cooley Distillery is not open to visitors. However, visitors are welcome to Locke's Distillery Museum at Kilbeggan 0900–1800 daily, Apr.–Oct., 1000–1600 Nov.–Mar. Groups please telephone in advance; tel: 0506-32134.

Like its stablemates Locke's, Tyrconnell and Inishowen, Kilbeggan was already a famous name before its recent relaunch by Cooley Distillery. The original whiskey was named after the village where Locke's Distillery stood, and in Gaelic meant 'little church' – a reference to a local medieval monastery. It is an apposite name for a whiskey, as monks were always the foremost distillers in every country across Europe. With the collective difficulties facing the Irish whiskey industry in the twentieth century, Locke's Distillery barely survived into the 1950s. But with the whiskies of the Cooley Distillery, the old Locke names and reputations are being revived, the warehouses once again hold maturing stocks and the distillery itself is being restored as a museum of industrial archaeology.

Locke's

Cooley Distillery,
Dundalk, Co. Louth

TYPE
Blend

STRENGTH
40%

TASTE RATING
2

MINIATURES
Yes

COMMENTS
Locke's is a smooth, superior-quality whiskey, whose malty sweetness is complemented by dryer, fresher notes.

VISITORS
Cooley Distillery is not open to visitors. However, visitors are welcome to Locke's Distillery Museum at Kilbeggan 0900–1800 daily, Apr.–Oct., 1000–1600 Nov.–Mar. Groups please telephone in advance; tel: 0506-32134

*A*nother revival from Cooley, Locke's was named after the nineteenth-century family-run distillery company. Licensed distilling began at the Kilbeggan site in 1757, and John Locke took over operations in 1843. The company remained successfully in business for over a century but by 1958, in common with much of Ireland's whiskey industry, receivership beckoned. After housing several business ventures the distillery came under the care of a local group until 1987, when the Locke company name was revived by the Cooley Distillery company who refurbished the warehouse and set up a cooperage. The old buildings are still being restored, and with equipment dating from Victorian times, the distillery itself is now a museum of industrial archaeology.

Midleton Very Rare

*Midleton Distillery,
Midleton, Co. Cork*

TYPE
Blend

STRENGTH
40%

TASTE RATING
3–4

MINIATURES
No

COMMENTS
The flavour emphasis of individual years varies, but the whiskey is characteristically smooth, with a malt sweetness and counterbalancing dry notes.

VISITORS
Visitors are welcome to The Jameson Heritage Centre at Midleton 1000–1800, Mar.–Oct. Telephone 021-613594.

*T*his whiskey is unusual in that it has been bottled annually since 1984, and each bottling is an event, limited to only several thousand individually numbered bottles. Distilling has been carried on at Midleton since 1825, when it was first established by the Murphy brothers (another branch of whose family began a brewery in Cork, still going strong). In 1868 the distillery joined the newly formed conglomerate of Cork Distilleries Co. and, almost a century later, the Irish Distillers Group. It survived the upheaval of both mergers, emerging as the single most important whiskey-production centre in Ireland. Over a dozen whiskies of varying traditions, tastes and characters are produced there, a testimony to the skill of its craftspeople.

Millars Special Reserve

Cooley Distillery, Dundalk, Co. Louth

TYPE

Blend

STRENGTH

40%

TASTE RATING

2–3

MINIATURES

No

COMMENTS

A smooth, nicely balanced blend which is sweet and fruity on the nose and in its flavours, with a complementary pleasing dryness.

VISITORS

Cooley Distillery is not open to visitors. However, visitors are welcome to Locke's Distillery Museum at Kilbeggan 0900–1800 daily, Apr.–Oct., 1000–1600 Nov.–Mar. Groups please telephone in advance; tel: 0506-32134.

*A*dam Millar & Co. was an old name in Dublin distilling, first established in 1843 and based near the Guinness brewery on the Liffey's south bank, and their whiskey was popular in Ireland, and particularly in Dublin, from the earlier part of the twentieth century right up to the 1970s. Adam Millar was bought over by the Cooley Distillery who have now relaunched Millars Special Reserve whiskey. Although on the market only since 1994, it is already an award winner. Eblana, a whiskey liqueur, has also now been launched under the Millar label, Eblana being an ancient Irish name for Dublin.

Millwood

Royal Cooymans B. V.,
Tilburg, The Netherlands

TYPE
Cream liqueur

STRENGTH
17%

TASTE RATING
2

MINIATURES
No

COMMENTS

A cream liqueur from the Netherlands, made with Dutch cream and Irish whiskey. Millwoods is a pleasant, non-cloying liqueur with chocolatey background flavours.

$\mathcal{R}$oyal Cooymans, producers of Millwood in the Netherlands, already had substantial experience in the liqueurs market as makers of advocaat before they began production of their Irish whiskey cream liqueur in 1980. The compnay has decided deliberately to reduce the cream and fat content of its liqueurs, and has reaped dividends in sales and professional recognition, winning awards for this and other drinks from its cream liqueurs range. Millwoods is also sold at 14% abv primarily for its home market in the Netherlands, as supermarkets there are not permitted to sell any alcohol above 15%.

O'Darby

J. J. O'Darby Ltd,
Dublin

TYPE
Cream liqueur

STRENGTH
17%

TASTE RATING
2

MINIATURES
No

COMMENTS
A mellow, caramel-sweet blend of Irish whiskey and spirits with cream and chocolate.

VISITORS
The plant is not open to visitors.

*A*nother of the Irish cream liqueurs to hit the market after the success of Baileys, O'Darby was originally made by a small local company before being bought by rival producers R. & J. Emmet; they in turn were bought by International Distillers and Vintners subsidiary Gilbey's in 1991. Emmets and The Dubliner cream liqueurs are produced alongside O'Darby, but the expertise at their Bailieboro plant means that the distinctive character and individual flavours of each brand is not only never compromised, but enhanced.

Paddy

*Midleton Distillery,
Midleton, Co. Cork*

TYPE
Blend

STRENGTH
40%

TASTE RATING
2

MINIATURES
Yes

COMMENTS
Paddy is light and fresh, almost sharp in its flavours, with a dry finish.

VISITORS
Visitors are welcome to The Jameson Heritage Centre at Midleton 1000–1800, Mar.–Oct. Telephone 021-613594.

Traditionally a Cork whiskey, Paddy is still the favoured brand of the south-west. It is now made by the Irish Distillers Group but its original owners were proclaimed in its unwieldy title, 'Cork Distilleries Company Old Irish Whiskey', a name which did not exactly flow from the tongue, or pen. In the 1910s the name began to be abandoned by Cork drinkers and publicans in favour of 'Paddy Flaherty's whiskey' – after an ebullient local rep. The full name eventually made its way onto the label, first at the foot then, simply as 'Paddy', as its main name. Cork Distilleries Co., themselves the result of an 1867 merger of a number of local distilleries, merged in 1966 into IDG, with their distillery at Midleton the one chosen as the group's production centre.

Power's

Midleton Distillery,
Midleton, Co. Cork

TYPE
Blend

STRENGTH
40%

TASTE RATING
3

MINIATURES
Yes

COMMENTS
A fresh, smooth Irish with fruity and malt flavours and a dry finish. This is the most popular of all Irish whiskies on the home market.

VISITORS
Visitors are welcome to The Jameson Heritage Centre at Midleton 1000–1800, Mar.–Oct. Telephone 021-613594.

*B*egun in 1791, Power & Son were one of the most far-sighted and successful Irish distillers of the nineteenth century. The company was responsible for some impressive marketing innovations, helping shape the whiskey market to a state recognisable today. In 1886 they became pioneers of bottling (then almost all drinks were sold from the barrel), protecting their product from adulteration, enhancing their name and emphasising their distinctiveness with the addition of a gold label still used on their whiskey today. Bottling also expanded the market by making whiskey portable to the home. Another first came with Powers' introduction of the miniature to the Irish market: a bottle had three swallows' capacity, and a celebratory visual pun is still seen on Powers' labels today.

Redbreast

Fitzgerald & Co. Ltd, Dublin

TYPE
Pot still

BOTTLING AGE
12 years

STRENGTH
40%

TASTE RATING
3

MINIATURES
No

COMMENTS
Redbreast is a classically Irish whiskey with an abundance of smooth, pot-still character. A difficult whiskey to find, even in Ireland.

*J*ameson's whiskies are the ones traditionally associated with this twelve years old, pure pot still Irish brand. It was first launched in 1939 for sale to whiskey merchants, but after Jameson's merger in 1966 into the Irish Distillers Group and subsequent move to Midleton Distillery in Co. Cork, stocks for Redbreast were no longer forthcoming. However, IDG recently decided to relaunch the brand themselves, through their Dublin-based vintners subsidiary Fitzgerald & Co. They are based in the IDG headquarters at Bow Street, in part of the old Jameson's distillery.

Royal Irish

*Royal Irish Distillery,
Belfast*

TYPE

Single distillery Irish malt

STRENGTH

Varies

TASTE RATING

3

MINIATURES

Yes

COMMENTS

A difficult-to-find whiskey sold only by independent bottlers, whose sweet, fragrant taste has counterbalancing drier notes and a pot-still backdrop.

*O*wned by the Dunville family, Belfast spirits merchants who decided to move into the whiskey-producing side of the business, the Royal Irish Distillery was built in 1869. Its products acquired a fine reputation, and the company's fortunes rode high in the late nineteenth and early twentieth century. The distillery also had the distinction of having its own, national-league-winning football team. But in the 1930s, having weathered the storms of domestic strife, US Prohibition and a world-wide depression, the company suffered a body-blow in the premature death of the last of the Dunville family. Rather than pursue an agressive sales approach to win new markets, the rest of the board voted to dissolve the company. Distilling resumed for only a brief period in the 1950s.

Sheridan's

Thomas Sheridan & Sons,
Dublin

TYPE
Cream liqueur

STRENGTH
17% (vanilla cream),
19.5% (coffee chocolate
liqueur)

TASTE RATING
2

MINIATURES
No

COMMENTS

Its white liqueur has a sooth-ing, white-chocolate richness, the black warming coffee and whiskey flavours and a round-ed, chocolatey-nutty finish. The whole is smooth and elegant, akin to a deliciously whiskied liquid *tiramisù*.

VISITORS

The plant is not open to visitors.

*U*isually stunning both on the shelf and in the glass, this award-winning cream liqueur is one of the most imaginative drinks ever produced. Not surprisingly, it is also the foremost impulse buy in the drinks market as a whole. Thomas Sheridan & Sons is owned by the Gilbey's group which produces, among others, Baileys, the world's top selling liqueur. Like its stable-mate, it is produced at the company's plant in Dublin, but unlike Baileys, Sheridan's was an instant success when it was launched on the cream liqueur market in early 1994. Sheri-dan's apparent gimmickry should not blind purchasers to the fact that this is a seriously good liqueur.

Tullamore

Tullamore Distillery,
Tullamore, Co. Offaly

TYPE

Single-distillery Irish whiskey

BOTTLING AGE

Varies

STRENGTH

Varies

TASTE RATING

3

MINIATURES

Yes

COMMENTS

A typically light but not spiritous whiskey with a fragrant,
sweet flavour.

*T*ullamore Distillery was founded in 1829, well placed in the
Midlands for distributing its produce
via the Grand Canal. Throughout its
history the distillery has been
renowned for producing the lightest
and most accessible of Irish whiskies,
a tradition carried on today. But with
the rest of the industry in Ireland,
Tullamore died a slow death into the
mid twentieth century. Its decline was
offset by the success of its Irish Mist
liqueur, but the distillery, still with
plenty of stocks, closed in 1954. Since
then it has been gradually demolished. Its products were bought by
Power & Son in 1965, passing with it
the following year into the Irish
Distillers Group. In 1994 the business
was sold on again to C&C International, part of Allied Domecq.

Tullamore Dew

Tullamore Dew Co. Ltd,
Tullamore, Co. Offaly

TYPE
Blend

STRENGTH
40%

TASTE RATING
2

MINIATURES
Yes

COMMENTS
A light, undemanding Irish blend with a smooth, sweet flavour. Good as an aperitif.

VISITORS
Tullamore Distillery is no longer operational, but visitors are welcome at The Jameson Heritage Cente at Midleton, where Tullamore Dew is produced, 1000–1800, Mar.–Oct. Telephone 021-613594.

*T*ullamore Distillery no longer exists as a wiskey-producing centre, but the name of its most famous whiskey lives on in a new incarnation which is one of the most popular Irish whiskies in Europe. The distillery was originally founded in 1829 by Michael Molloy, but by the late 1880s was under the co-ownership and control of Daniel E. Williams, who had worked at the distillery from his boyhood. His initials were the inspiration for the name of the company's most famous product and, in turn, for the deathless advertising slogan still featured on every bottle, 'Give Every Man His Dew'. The distillery fell victim to the recession in the Irish whiskey industry in the mid twentieth century, and today Tullamore Dew is produced in Co. Cork at Midleton Distillery.

Tyrconnell

Cooley Distillery,
Dundalk, Co. Louth

TYPE

Single malt

STRENGTH

40%

TASTE RATING

2–3

MINIATURES

Yes

COMMENTS

The Tyrconnell is smooth, mellow whiskey whose light and sweet taste is complemented by a pleasingly dry finish.

VISITORS

Cooley Distillery is not open to visitors. However, visitors are welcome to Locke's Distillery Museum at Kilbeggan 0900–1800 daily, Apr.–Oct., 1000–1600 Nov.–Mar. Groups please telephone in advance; tel: 0506-32134.

*T*oday produced at the Cooley Distillery, this whiskey was once the prime brand of the Londonderry distillery of A. A. Watt & Co., which was bought out and closed by the Scottish Distillers Company Ltd in 1925. The original Tyrconnell was one of the most popular Irish whiskies in the early twentieth century, and was therefore a fitting candidate for revival recently by its new owners, John Locke & Co. In 1876 the name Tyrconnell was borne by a horse which was owned by the Watt family and entered in the Irish classic race, 'The Queen Victoria Plate'. The horse's victory and its dream odds are still celebrated on its namesake's label today.

Appendix 1:
Developing the Palate
by Una Holden-Cosgrove

*A*part from the anatomical meaning – the roof of the mouth – a palate refers to the sense of taste, but the roof of the mouth does play an important role in discerning a taste. Spicy, hot and cold, pleasant and objectionable sensations are all in the province of the palate. Everyone has a different reaction to taste and both physically and psychologically the sense of smell has a major influence on how these sensations are perceived.

Where whisky is concerned, a palate needs to be educated in the same way as it must gradually be introduced to the different foods encountered in different countries – after all, a vindaloo is hardly the best introduction to curries! Similarly, a dram of one whisky can never be regarded as a real experience or a satisfactory introduction to the elixir of life. Every whisky has a different taste and smell: some are quite fierce, or vigorous, and others more honeyed and enticing. To attempt one of the more powerful malts, such as The Glenlivet or Talisker, without any previous knowledge of whisky can only kill any interest in proceeding further.

Unfortunately the early writers on whisky overlooked the fact that their palates were accustomed to the differing tastes and had been conditioned so that the robust types were more to their particular liking. As a result the malts and blends they recommended so highly were usually too powerful for the beginner, leading to an undeservedly macho image for malt whisky which meant that these stronger whiskies were more commonly found on the shelves of bars outside Scotland.

An ideal way to demonstrate this difference in taste is used at whisky-tasting sessions, where the participants are gently guided through a series of malts, starting with the softer, fruity smelling ones and slowly working through to the stronger ones. With this manipulation of the palate, almost invariably the participants find the final dram the most appealing! As these participants do not always appreciate that the aim of tastings is to show how good even the stronger malts are when the palate has been tutored, they are liable to seek out the strongest one to try again at a later date, only to find it tastes too strong – their palate has not really developed sufficiently to cope with it without more experience. So how should a palate be developed?

It is perhaps advisable to start with a whisky mix, as long as the whisky is a blend, or a grain such as Invergordon, and not a malt. Lemonade, soda, even water and ice are possible mixes for blended whisky. This will begin to train the senses and on cold days a Whisky Mac (blended whisky and Green Ginger) will provide a feeling of warmth that goes hand in hand with other pleasant sensations. A really fine blend – such as Black Bottle – can then be attempted neat.

Graduation to a malt requires good company and careful thought. For most beginners the spirit should not assail the taste buds, but inveigle the senses through an appealing scent, subtle taste and soothing after-effects. The aroma, which should be savoured before a sip is taken, can be spicy,

fruity, flowery or peaty, and as with other scents]
and aftershave, individual preferences must be
The taste for the inexperienced should not be fierce – instead,
the malt should be chosen from among the smooth, velvety
and honeyed selections. Some are dry and others a little
sweet, and once again personal preference must be recognized.

After-effects are every bit as important, as the palate can be
attacked some time after a stronger malt has been imbibed,
and this can be unpleasant to the unwary. There are a variety
of exciting after-effects that should be experienced and appreciated. The sparkles on the tongue and roof of the mouth provided by such malts as Oban and Aberlour are quite delightful, the feeling of being massaged, not just in the mouth but
all over the shoulders and back, as produced by such as
Glendullan after only one sip will help to cure most stress
reactions. There are sensations of glowing warmth in the
mouth, further reminiscent tastes of fruit or other pleasant
foods and even a very delayed sharpness that comes as an
unexpected surprise.

The use of miniatures is extremely helpful in identifying
whiskies that appeal most to an individual. Further tutoring
of the palate should be by experiencing the stronger ones in
graduated steps, rather than by assaulting an unprepared and
unsuspecting mouth!

Very simply, to drink a malt whisky properly, in order to
obtain maximum enjoyment, it is necessary to consider the
smell, taste and after-effects that would appeal to a particular
individual. Time should be spent appreciating the aroma, tak-

ing only a small sip, letting it roll around the mouth before swallowing it and then awaiting the enjoyment of its after-effects. It is also well to remember that mood and the time of day as well as the weather conditions play a role in palate appeal. What may at the end of a horrible day seem like the most wonderful malt on earth, could well appear boring and inadequate on a cold winter's night or overwhelming in the middle of a happy gathering on a glorious summer's after-noon. Remember, too, that a palate will change with experi-ence.

There are many, many blends, a few grain whiskies, a num-ber of vatted malts and about 160 single malts (from approxi-mately 120 distilleries, with some producing more than one year and volume) from which to choose. All are different, each with a different effect on different palates and providing the customer with a wonderful choice and opportunity to learn about a fascinating topic. If the beginner treats whisky with respect, the experiences encountered in the process of development will prove enchanting.

Appendix 2:
Personal Tasting Record

All the whiskies featured in this book are listed below. As you try each one, record a mark out of 10, in terms of personal enjoyment according to your own tastes and preferences, and so build up a personalised tasting log.

Scotch

	Aberfeldy		Benriach
	Aberlour		Benrinnes
	An Cnoc		Benromach
	The Antiquary		Big "T"
	Ardbeg		Black & White
	Ardmore		Black Bottle
	Auchentoshan		Bladnoch
	Aultmore		Blair Athol
	Bailie Nicol Jarvie		Bowmore
	Balblair		Bruichladdich
	Ballentine's		Bunnahabhain
	Balmenach		Cameron Brig
	The Balvenie		Caol Ila
	Banff		Caperdonich
	Bell's Extra Special		Cardhu
	Ben Nevis		Chivas Regal

The Claymore	The Famous Grouse
Clynelish	Fraser McDonald
Coleburn	Glayva
Columba Cream	Glen Albyn
Convalmore	Glenburgie
Cragganmore	Glencadam
Craigellachie	Glen Calder
Crawford's 3-Star	Glen Deveron
Cutty Sark	Glendronach
Cutty Sark Emerald	Glendullan
Cutty Sark Imperial Kingdom Golden Jubilee	Glenfarclas
Dailuaine	Glenfiddich
The Dalmore	Glen Garioch
Dalwhinnie	Glengoyne
Deanston	Glen Grant
Dewar's White Label	Glen Keith
Dimple	Glenkinchie
Drambuie	The Glenlivet
Dufftown	Glenlochy
Dunhill	Glenlossie
Dunkeld Atholl Brose	Glen Mhor
The Edradour	Glenmorangie
Fairlie's	Glenmorangie Port Wood
	Glen Moray

☐	Glen Ord	☐	Johnnie Wal
☐	Glen Rosa	☐	Johnnie Walker Blue Lab
☐	The Glen Rothes	☐	Johnnie Walker Red Label
☐	Glen Scotia	☐	Knockando
☐	Glentauchers	☐	Lagavulin
☐	The Glenturret	☐	Laphroaig
☐	The Glenturret Original Malt Liqueur	☐	Lauder's
☐	Glenugie	☐	Ledaig
☐	Grand Macnish	☐	Linkwood
☐	Haig	☐	Littlemill
☐	Heather Cream	☐	The Loch Fyne
☐	Highland Park	☐	Loch Ranza
☐	Immortal Memory	☐	Lochside
☐	Imperial	☐	Long John
☐	Inchgower	☐	Longmorn
☐	Inchmurrin	☐	Longrow
☐	Invergordon	☐	The Macallan
☐	Inverleven	☐	Stewart Macduff
☐	Island Prince	☐	Millburn
☐	Islay Mist	☐	Miltonduff
☐	Isle of Jura	☐	Mortlach
☐	J&B Rare	☐	North Port
☐	J&B Jet	☐	Oban
		☐	Old Fettercairn

	Old Parr		Stewarts Cream of the Barley
	100 Hundred Pipers		Strathisla
	The Original Mackinlay		Talisker
	Passport		Tamdhu
	Pinwinnie		Tamnavulin
	Pittyvaich		Teacher's Highland Cream
	Port Ellen		Teaninich
	Pride of Islay		Tobermory
	Pride of the Lowlands		Tomatin
	Pride of Orkney		Tomintoul
	Pride of Strathspey		The Tormore
	Pulteney		Tullibardine
	Rosebank		Ultima
	Royal Brackla		VAT 69
	Royal Culross		White Horse
	Royal Lochnagar		Whyte & Mackay
	St Magdalene		William Grant
	Scapa		
	Scotia Royale		
	The Singleton of Auchroisk		
	Speyburn		
	Springbank		
	Stag's Breath Liqueur		